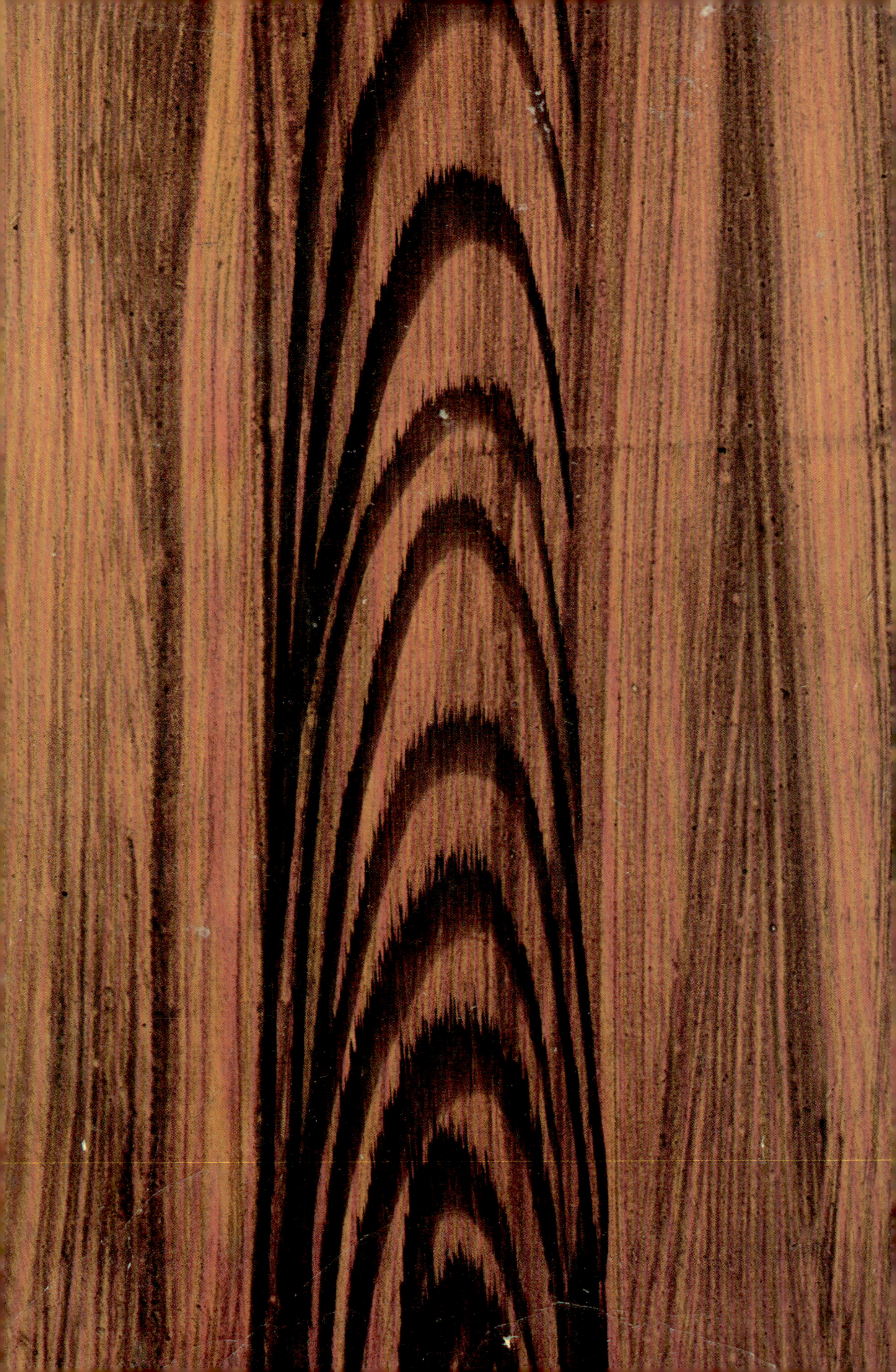

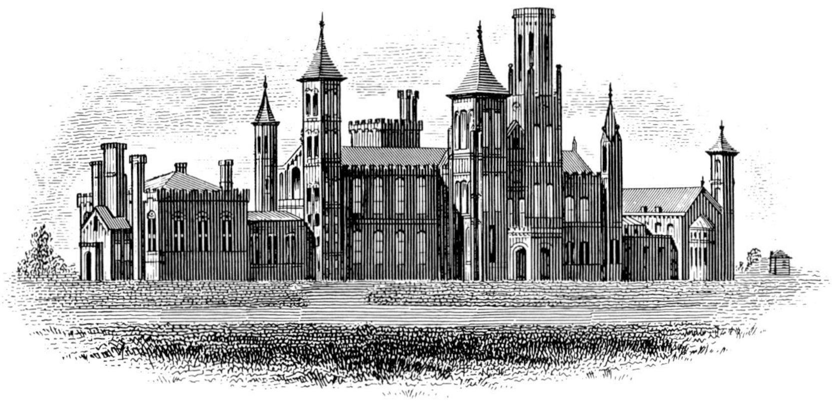

Smithsonian Institution Libraries
Branch Libraries

Anacostia Museum Branch Library

Anthropology Branch Library, National Museum of Natural History

Botany Branch Library, National Museum of Natural History

Central Reference and Loan Services Branch Library

Cooper-Hewitt, National Design Museum Branch Library

Dibner Library of the History of Science and Technology

Harvard-Smithsonian Center for Astrophysics Branch Library

Horticulture Branch Library

Museum Reference Center

Museum Support Center Branch Library

National Air and Space Museum Branch Library

National Museum of African Art Branch Library

National Museum of American History Branch Library

National Museum of Natural History Branch Library

National Postal Museum Branch Library

National Zoological Park Branch Library

Smithsonian Environmental Research Center Branch Library

Smithsonian Tropical Research Institute Branch Library

Rare Books and Special Collections

IN THE

Smithsonian Institution Libraries

W A S H I N G T O N · M C M X C V

Library of Congress Cataloging-in-Publication Data

Smithsonian Institution. Libraries.

Rare books and special collections in the Smithsonian Institution Libraries

p. cm.

Includes bibliographical references.

ISBN 1-56098-625-5

1. Smithsonian Institution. Libraries. 2. Library resources — Washington (D.C.) I. Wells, Ellen B. II. Overstreet, Leslie K. III. Title. IV. Title: Smithsonian Institution Libraries

Z0733.S67S64 1995 95-6791

026'973 — dc20 CIP

Cover: "*Prunus maritima racemosa, folio rotundo glabro; fructu minore purpureo.* The Mangrove Grape Tree." Mark Catesby. *The natural history of Carolina, Florida and the Bahama Islands.* London, 1731–43

Back Cover: "A balloon prospect above the clouds." Thomas Baldwin. *Airopaidia: containing the narrative of a balloon excursion from Chester, the eighth of September 1785.* Chester [England], 1786. Gift of the Burndy Library.

Endleaves: "King wood" and "Cedar." William Mullingar Higgins. *The house painter: or, decorator's companion.* London, 1841. From the Robert D. Mussey, Jr. collection.

One of many technical works on nineteenth-century craftsmanship in the Libraries' collections, this volume contains hand-painted illustrations of various wood grains along with descriptions of how to achieve each effect. It was written for craftsmen, architects, and interior designers, and the illustrations in this copy, with their spatters and stains, show heavy use in the workshop.

Contents

Foreword—7

Introduction—12

GENERAL KNOWLEDGE—22

MUSEUMS—27

Early science museums . . . Scientific collecting and conservation . . . Smithsoniana

PHYSICAL SCIENCES AND MATHEMATICS—35

Mathematics . . . Mapping the earth and heavens

EARTH SCIENCES—43

Geology and minerals . . . Paleontology

TECHNOLOGY, INDUSTRY, ENGINEERING—49

Electrical engineering and magnetism . . . Mechanical and civil engineering . . . Flight . . . World's fairs and international expositions . . . Trade literature

NATURAL HISTORY—68

Zoology . . . Botany . . . Voyages and expeditions

CULTURAL AND SOCIAL HISTORY—86

American history and life . . . African art . . . Juvenile literature

ANTHROPOLOGY—94

Native American studies . . . Missionary publications . . . Central and Latin America

DECORATIVE ARTS—103

Interior design . . . Landscape design

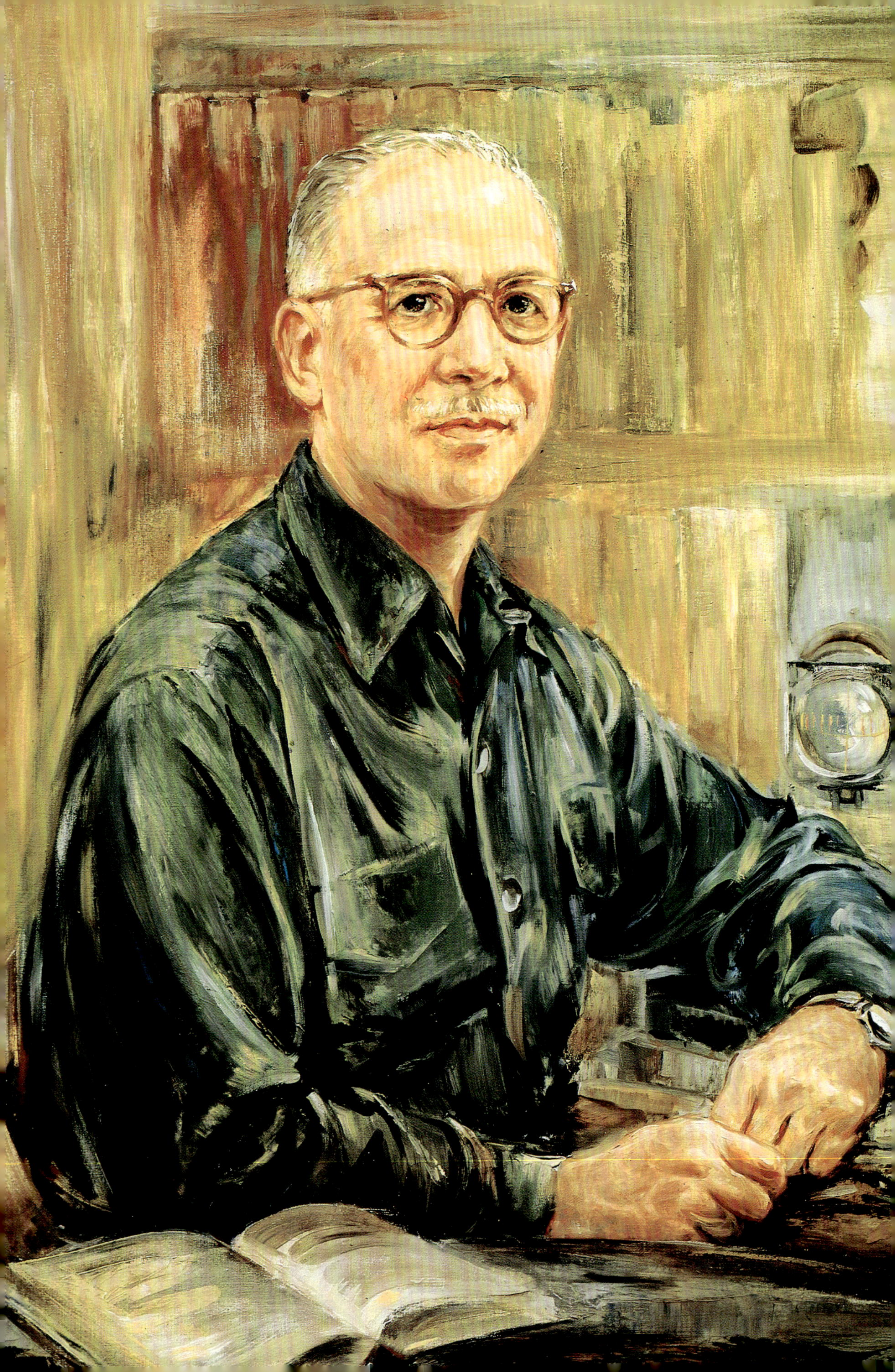

Foreword

LIBRARIES AT THE SMITHSONIAN DATE FROM ITS FOUNDING. The eighteen branches that now comprise the Smithsonian Institution Libraries hold collections that support the museums and research centers that embrace the Institution's nineteenth-century mandate for "the increase and diffusion of knowledge." Those items of special or unusual value are separately provided for as special collections.

Through the years the Special Collections of the Institution libraries have benefited from the generosity of many people. Curators have donated their personal libraries, adding to the enviable strengths of the collections in the history of science and technology, the wide-ranging fields of natural history, and the Institution's more recent interests in social and cultural history and the fine arts. Gifts from individuals and institutions as well as transfers from government offices have enriched the collections. The Special Collections Department cares for these rare and special materials. We hope that you will learn enough from this publication about the scope and depth of these collections to appreciate how they contribute to the Smithsonian's ongoing work in its research, exhibition, publication, and education programs.

In 1976 The Dibner Library of the History of Science and Technology was established with the gift from the Burndy Library of Norwalk, Connecticut, created by Dr. Bern Dibner. The gift provided the Libraries with its first rare book library, located in the National Museum of American History. A rare book library is planned for the National Museum of Natural History to house and preserve the many natural history books dispersed among a number of locations. This new facility will ensure that the Special Collections Department will provide improved care for the materials in its charge, and be better able to accept the gifts which continue to come, building on the strengths of these splendid collections. Other locations housing Special Collections materials are the Admiral DeWitt Clinton Ramsey Room in the National Air and Space Museum Branch Library, the Bradley Room in the Cooper-Hewitt National Design Museum Branch Library, and the Jewett Room in the Arts and Industries Building.

Nearly all the items in Special Collections are cataloged, and information about them is available through national and international online databases affording the scholarly community the opportunity to learn of these rich resources. The increasing value of the collections reminds us continually of our

---

Bern Dibner. Digital color reproduction of an oil portrait signed Lucerne Robert, 1957, in the collection of David Dibner.

obligation to provide the best care and security for these materials. Our responsibility to ensure that generations of researchers will benefit from the knowledge contained in them drives our concern for conservation and preservation as well.

We are pleased to offer this introduction to the Special Collections of the Smithsonian Institution Libraries and invite you to browse through it. We also invite you to visit the Libraries' Exhibition Gallery and consult our collections as your research needs require. We welcome, indeed, encourage, gifts of rare books as well as contributions to the Smithsonian Institution Libraries Special Collections Endowment and Preservation Program.

Support for this publication was provided by The Dibner Fund.

Barbara J. Smith
Director
December 1994

Opposite: Sebastianus David Louys. *Gheometria oft de konste van landt te meten* [Geometry, or the best way to measure land]. Manuscript, 1681. Gift of the Burndy Library.

This manuscript is an anthology by a student-scholar and includes notes on geometry, land measurement, and surveying, illustrated with pen-and-ink drawings. Written mostly in Dutch, portions are in Latin and French.

Pages 10–11: Interior of the Charles Coffin Jewett Room, Arts and Industries Building, Smithsonian Institution (1993).

Puntten umbræ rectæ (d'welck nochtans selden kan gebeuren) genomen int het eirste staen, vallet loot op 80 puncten, ende het tweede staen 25 umb: rectæ. Soo trecht 25 van 80 ende gij sult hebben 55 voor uwen divis: ende die distantie tuijsschen die 2 sta=tien is 32 voeten nu multg: 32 met 80 puncten ende sal komẽ 2560 die deelt door 55 en sal #

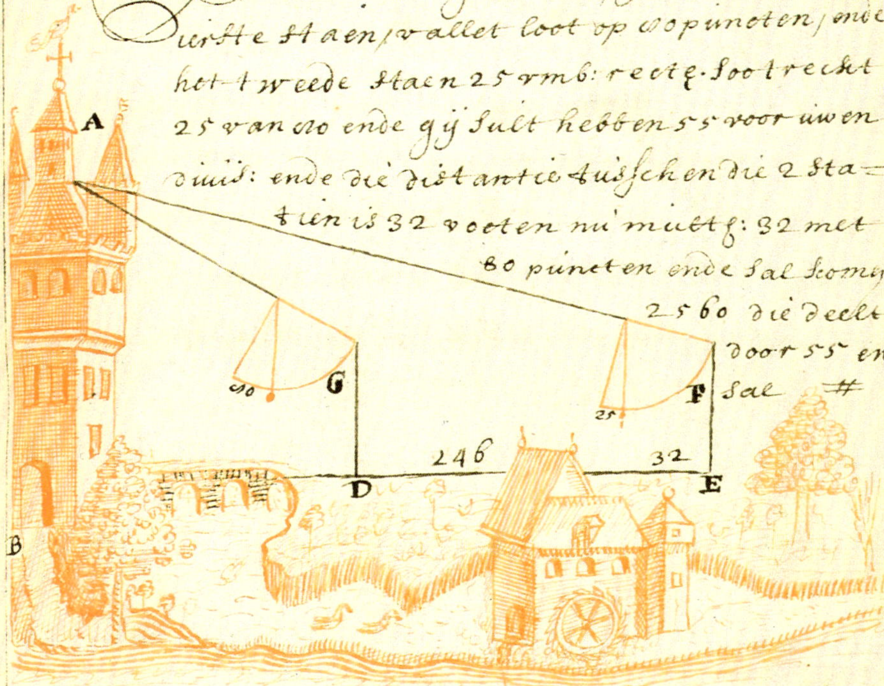

komen $46\frac{6}{11}$ die hooghde des torens, als gij de lenghde van uwe oge daer toe addeert.

Ende oft nu geviel dat int eerste staen het loot valt op $91\frac{2}{3}$ puncten umbræ rectæ, ende int ander op $83\frac{1}{3}$ umbræ versæ soo suldij deelen duijsent (want dat is numerus quadratus vijft hondert puncten) met $83\frac{1}{3}$, en vuijt dier divi=sien sal komen 120. ende dit en is ander met

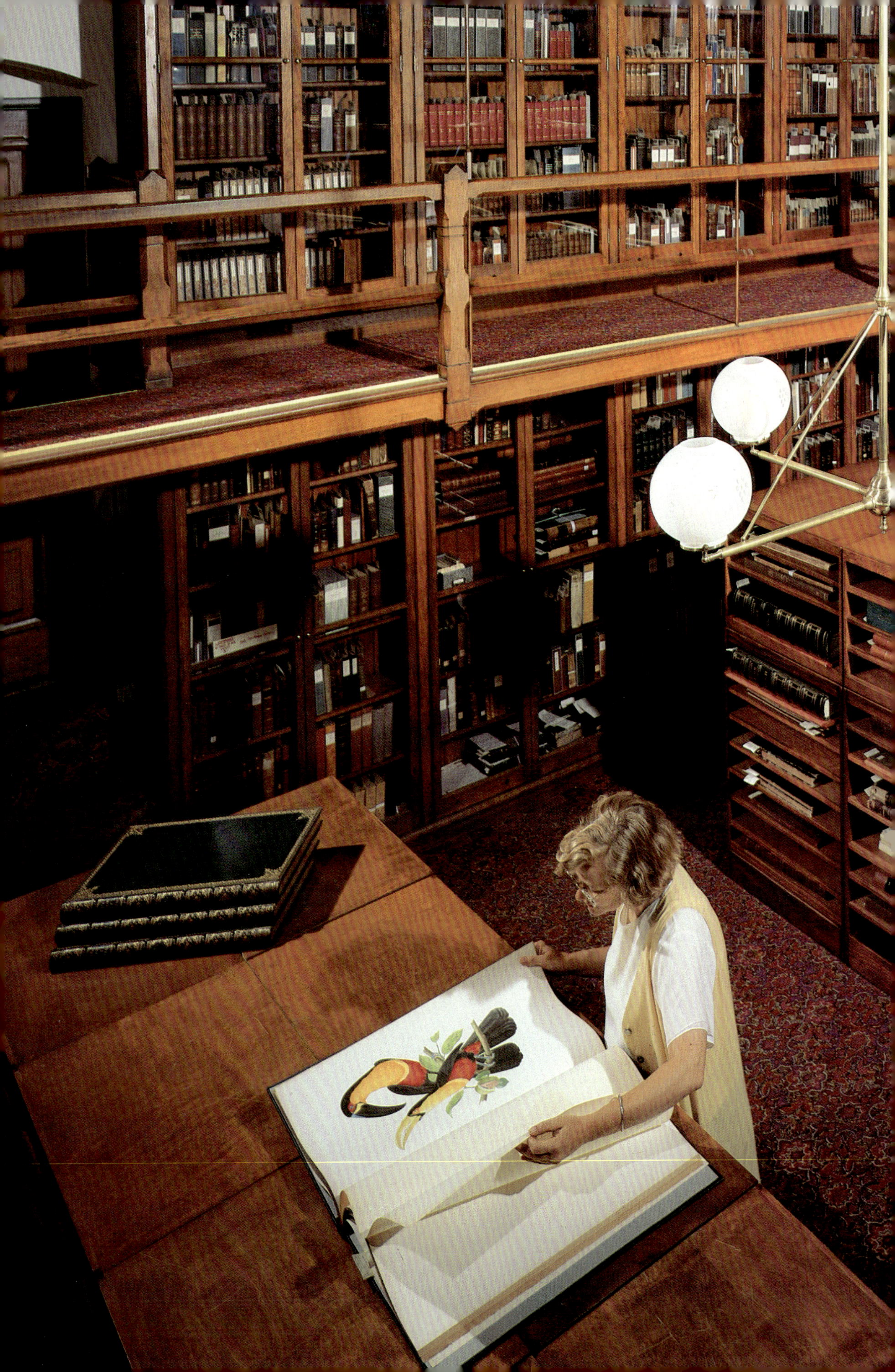

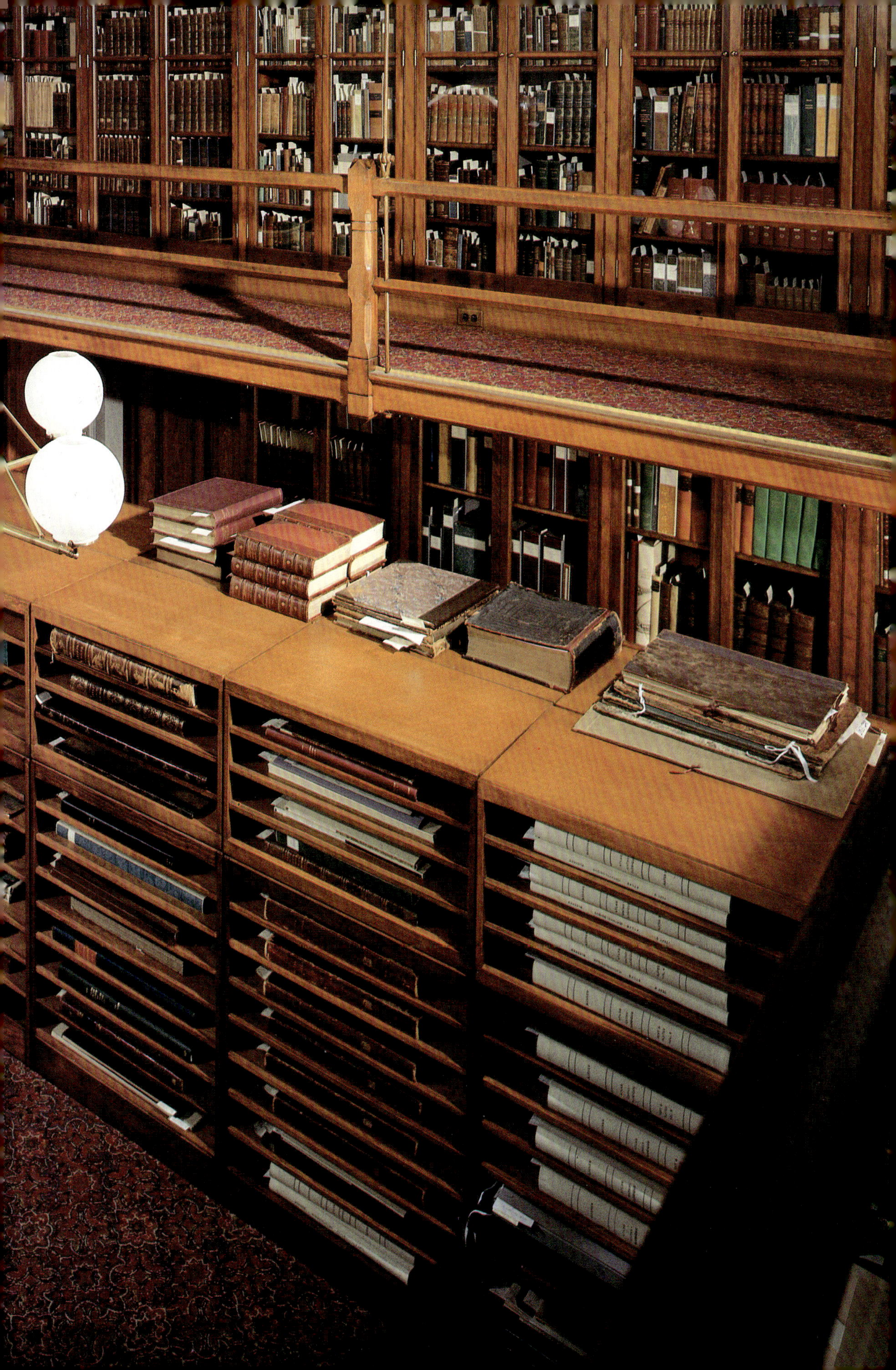

Introduction

THE SPECIAL COLLECTIONS OF THE SMITHSONIAN INSTITUTION Libraries are among its most intriguing and unusual assets. They comprise books, journals, and pamphlets as well as manuscripts, maps, prints, artifacts, and the surviving volumes of James Smithson's personal library. Because of their rarity, cost, beauty, unusual content, form, or physical condition, these works all demand the best possible storage environment and highest security. The Special Collections contain 40,000 rare and valuable volumes and 1,800 manuscript groups, the majority dating from the fifteenth to the eighteenth centuries. Another component consists of 285,600 trade catalogs and related printed materials which document the history of American technology, manufacturing, and business. The Libraries also houses an extensive collection of publications relating to world's fairs and international expositions.

The Smithsonian Institution owes its existence to the benevolence of an Englishman, James Smithson (1765–1829), who left an estate worth over $500,000 to the United States of America to create in Washington an institution "for the increase and diffusion of knowledge." Joseph Henry, a prominent physical scientist and the Institution's first Secretary (the title designated in the enabling legislation), interpreted this mandate broadly to include all areas of knowledge. He wished to use the income from the bequest principally to sponsor original research and to publish the results in a series of volumes established as the *Smithsonian Contributions to Knowledge.* When the first volume appeared, Henry set up a wide-ranging program of domestic distribution and international exchange, with the intention of gathering a complete set of the transactions and proceedings from scientific and literary societies all over the world. Henry's successful exchange program and a copyright deposit provision in the founding legislation stimulated a quick expansion of a library at the Smithsonian, which grew to 40,000 volumes by 1866. When the library's growth threatened to engulf Henry's other efforts, he succeeded in persuading Congress to revoke the

---

Willem Piso. *Historia naturalis brasiliæ* [The natural history of Brazil]. Leyden and Amsterdam, 1648. Gift of Marcia Brady Tucker.

Piso (1611–1678) was a pioneer of tropical medicine, studying the pharmacopeia of Native Americans; he first brought to Western attention such plants as sarsaparilla and sassafras. Piso's descriptions of new species in this early account of the natural history of Brazil are cited extensively by Linnaeus in establishing scientific names. Georg Marcgraf (1610–1644) collected zoological and botanical specimens and wrote the natural history sections of the book.

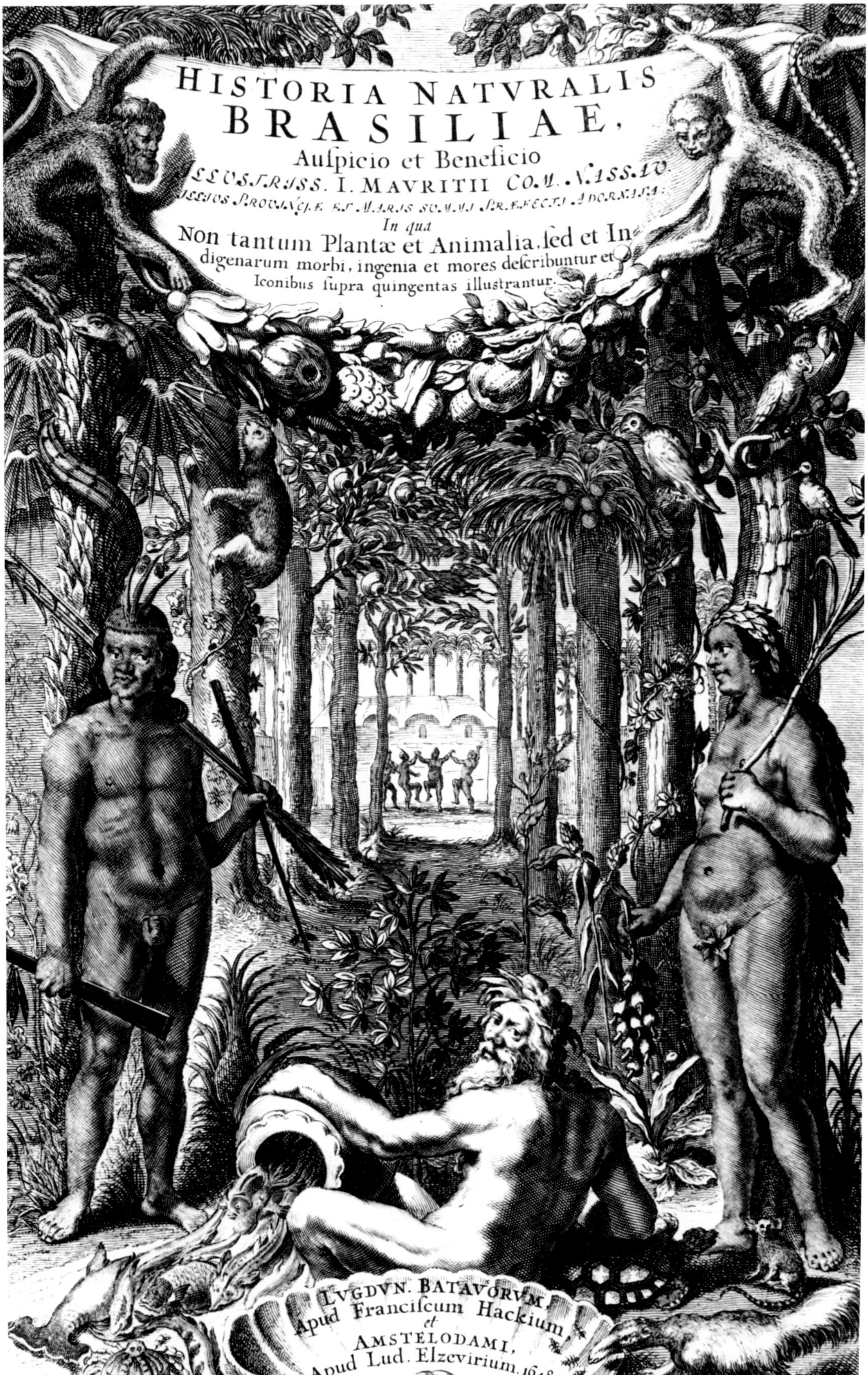
HISTORIA NATVRALIS
BRASILIAE,
Auſpicio et Beneficio
ILLUSTRISS. I. MAURITII COM. NASSAU
ILLIUS PROVINCIAE ET MARIS SUMMI PRAEFECTI ADORNATA:
In qua
Non tantum Plantæ et Animalia, ſed et Indigenarum morbi, ingenia et mores deſcribuntur et
Iconibus ſupra quingentas illuſtrantur.
LUGDUN. BATAVORUM,
Apud Franciſcum Hackium,
et
AMSTELODAMI,
Apud Lud. Elzevirium. 1648.

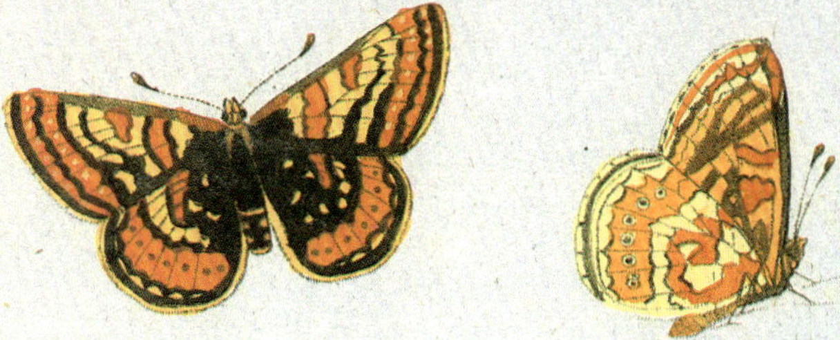

Papilio S. Artemis Fabr.

copyright deposit condition. Later, following a serious fire in one part of the Castle, the Smithsonian's building on the Mall, Henry arranged to move the Institution's library to fireproof space in the Library of Congress.

Henry's successor, Secretary Spencer F. Baird, re-created a library at the Smithsonian, donating for its foundation his own extensive private collection of books and other works. As Baird intensified the pace of the Institution's museum and collection activities, the Smithsonian systematically acquired more reference books for the study and curation of museum objects and specimens. Baird's efforts, coupled with numerous substantial gifts, helped to rebuild the library's holdings, which today number over 1.2 million volumes.

The diversity of subject matter collected by the Libraries matches the range of disciplines and activities undertaken by Smithsonian researchers and affiliated staff since the founding of the Institution. The world's fair collection, for example, grew largely from the Smithsonian's activity as organizer and participant in many of the fairs prior to the First World War. The natural history collections of books, journals, and manuscripts, dating from the eighteenth century, were acquired to assist in the study and care of the Institution's extensive specimen collections. The Smithsonian's scope of interest has expanded over the past 150 years, and new museums and research entities have emerged from the parent body. The related museum collections and library materials have followed as new parts of the Smithsonian separated and established their own identities.

The United States National Museum was established within the Institution in 1858, when the Smithsonian accepted its first collections of specimens. In 1881, a red-brick edifice now known as the Arts and Industries Building was completed next to the Castle to accommodate many of the overflowing collections of the growing National Museum and a library. A grand new building, the third United States National Museum, opened in 1910 on the Mall opposite the Castle to house the natural history collections. A few miles away in Rock Creek Park the National Zoological Park was formed in 1889. By 1969 the United States National Museum was formally divided into the National Museum of Natural History and the National Museum of History and Technology; the latter was housed in a new building that, in 1980, was renamed the National Museum of American History. A decorative arts and design museum was added when the Cooper-Hewitt joined the Institution in 1976. In the twentieth century, separate entities devoted entirely to scientific investigations in astronomy, tropical ecosystems, and environmental research were created along with laboratories for conservation and molecular systematics. In more recent years, specialized

---

"*Papilio s. Artemis* Fabr." Georg Wolfgang Franz Panzer. *Faunæ insectorum germanicæ initia* [The elements of the German insect fauna]. Nuremberg, 1796–1813.

A plate from Panzer, drawn actual size and etched by entomological artist Jakob Sturm.

museums for African art, postal history, and (anticipated) museums for Native Americans and African Americans have introduced new emphases.

The library collections have grown and divided accordingly. In 1968, Secretary S. Dillon Ripley established at the Smithsonian a library system uniting many of the museum and research center libraries into one comprehensive operation. Collections development, acquisition, and technical processing functions and research services operations were centralized and, since that decree, the Smithsonian Institution Libraries has grown to encompass eighteen branch libraries.* The Libraries' collections are used by researchers to identify and document the vast artifact and specimen collections in what has become the largest complex of museums and research centers in the world. Connected by an intricate web of communications networks, the branch libraries also support the research of scholars within and outside the Institution and members of the Smithsonian's exhibition, program, press, magazine, legal, and administrative staff.

The collecting policy for the Libraries reflects this broad focus. Reference works consulted by working scientists in the mid-nineteenth century now qualify as Special Collections materials because of their age and present rarity. The Libraries continues to acquire specialized works, avoiding duplicating items owned by other libraries in the Washington metropolitan area. The Special Collections are housed in locations that allow for convenient use by the Smithsonian researchers most closely affiliated with the subjects. The Dibner Library of the History of Science and Technology, located in the National Museum of American History, holds approximately 18,000 volumes and 1,800 manuscript units, including the Libraries' most substantial gift of rare materials from a single donor. In 1976, the Burndy Library in Norwalk, Connecticut, gave to the Smithsonian approximately 8,000 books, manuscripts, printed portraits, artifacts, and commemorative medals, the product of the collecting expertise and zeal of electrical engineer Bern Dibner, founder of The Burndy Corporation. With support from The Dibner Fund, the Smithsonian Institution Libraries

* Three other libraries within the Smithsonian are separate from the Smithsonian Institution Libraries system: they serve the Freer Gallery of Art and Arthur M. Sackler Gallery, the Hirshhorn Museum and Sculpture Garden, and the National Museum of American Art and National Portrait Gallery.

Michel Eugène Chevreul. *De la loi du contraste simultane des couleurs* [On the law of simultaneous contrast of colors]. Paris, 1889. Gift of Harvey Smith.

A chemist and director of dyeing at the Manufactures Royales des Gobelins (the national tapestry workshop), Chevreul studied the laws of color, contrast, and figure/ground effects. This is his best-known publication and a seminal contribution to color theory, influencing the Impressionists Georges Seurat, Claude Monet, and Paul Signac. In this lithographed illustration, each dot is colored by hand.

Fig. 89.

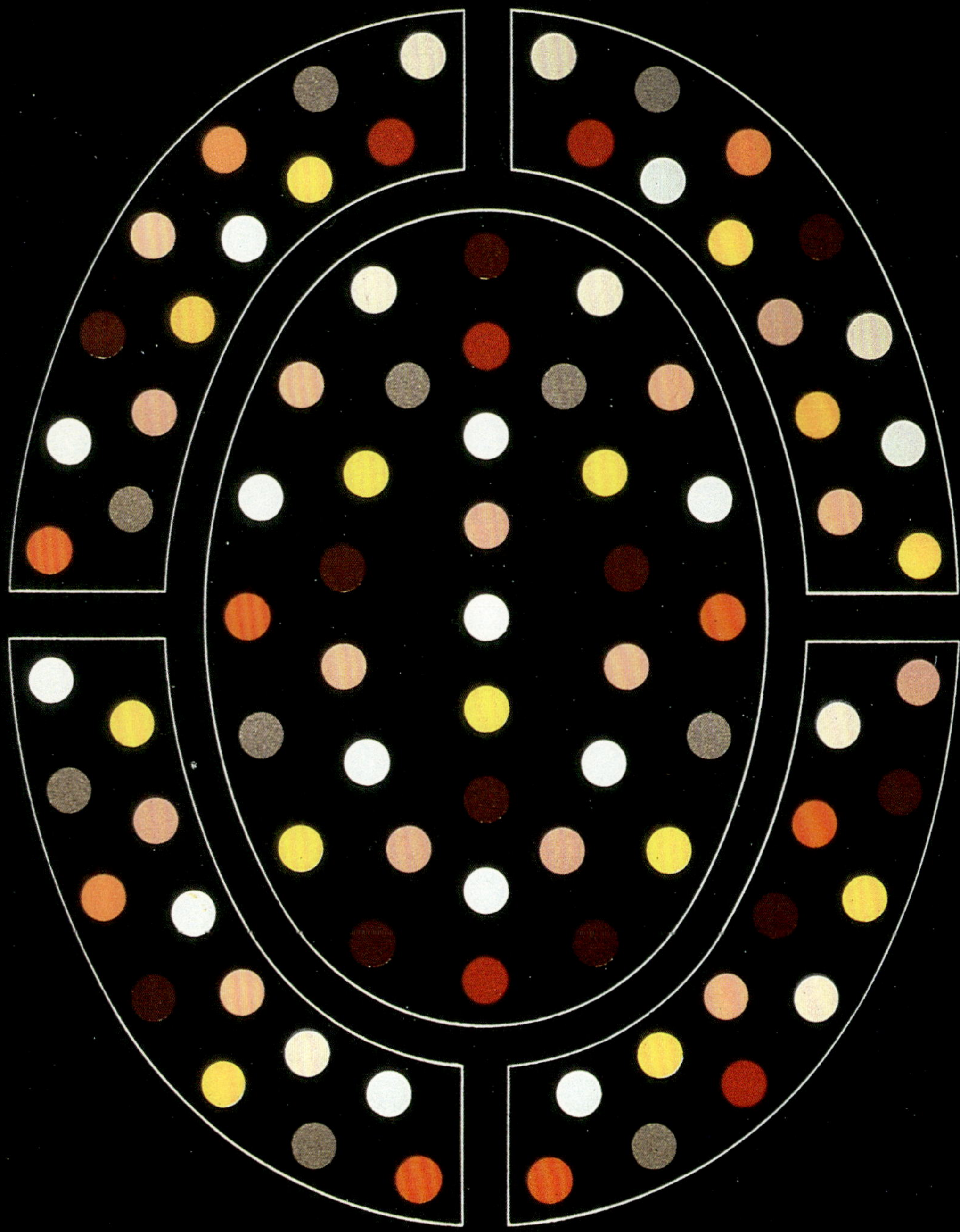

Paradigma terrae plagas 4. ac 12 ventorum situm indicans.

Pentastichon

Variarum mensurarum rationem indicans.

quatuor ex granis digitus componitur unus
Est quater in palmo digitus: quater in pede palmus:
Quinque pedes passum faciunt: passus quoque centum
viginti quinque stadium dant: sed miliare
octo dabunt stadia: duplicatum dat tibi Leuca.

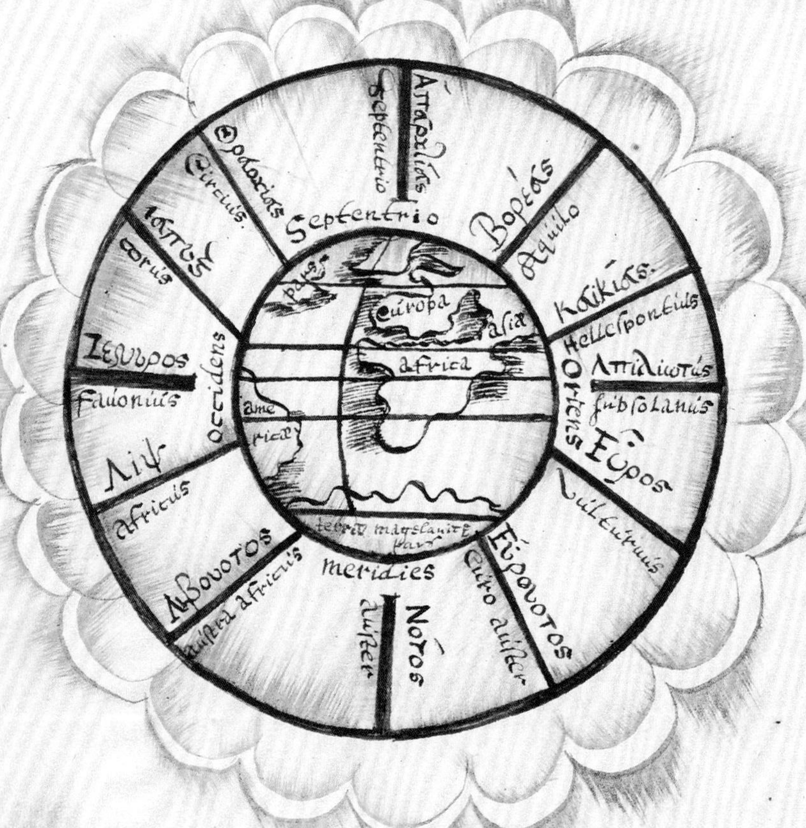

presents an annual lecture on a scientific subject that relates to the Burndy donation. Since 1992, the Fund has also supported the Smithsonian Institution Libraries/Dibner Library Resident Scholar Program to encourage the use of the Dibner Library collection for research in the history of science and technology.

Substantive portions of the Special Collections are housed in other Smithsonian Libraries' branches. At the Smithsonian's Cooper-Hewitt National Design Museum in New York City, the Bradley Room (named for Mr. and Mrs. Thomas A. Bradley) contains an extensive collection of works on American and European decorative arts and design. The Admiral DeWitt Clinton Ramsey Room at the National Air and Space Museum focuses on the history of flight and includes special collections of sheet music and juvenile literature which display the impact of aviation on popular culture. The National Museum of Natural History is providing space for a rare book facility as part of a major construction project now on the drawing board; upon completion, the Libraries will consolidate its extensive collection of rare and valuable natural history volumes at this location.

We present here a pictorial introduction to the Special Collections. It is not a comprehensive guide, nor does it focus on the conventionally recognized rare works in the various subjects treated. Rather it is a sampler in subject areas that are especially strong, and intentionally it stresses aspects of the collection that are unusual or distinctive to the Smithsonian.

Bibliographic records for the individual works are available through two international databases of library holdings, OCLC (Online Computer Library Center) and RLIN (Research Libraries Information Network). Records are also available through SIRIS, the Smithsonian Institution Research Information System, which is accessible through the Internet. Readers may wish to consult the following published works:

Bern Dibner, *Heralds of science.* Rev. ed. Norwalk, Conn.: Burndy Library, and Washington, D.C.: Smithsonian Institution, 1980.

Manuscripts of the Dibner Collection. Washington, D.C.: Smithsonian Institution Libraries, 1985.

The books of the fairs; materials about world's fairs, 1834–1916, in the Smithsonian Institution Libraries. Chicago: American Library Association, 1992.

"Paradigma terræ plagas 4. de ventorum situ indicans" [Model indicating the sites of the winds in the four zones of earth]. Cornelius van Nederven. *Annotata physicalia* [Annotations on natural philosophy]. [Breda?], 1657–58. Manuscript in Latin and Dutch. Gift of the Burndy Library.

Nederven, a student in Breda, compiled this volume of over 400 pages minutely inscribed with excerpts from the works of Aristotle and Joannes de Sacro Bosco, among others, on the form of the world. This drawing shows the ancient Greek depiction of the four winds imposed on the seventeenth-century version of world geography.

Betty Jo Teeter Dobbs, *Alchemical death & resurrection; the significance of alchemy in the age of Newton.* Washington, D.C.: Smithsonian Institution Libraries, 1990. Illustrated lecture based on a manuscript by Sir Isaac Newton that is part of the Burndy Library's gift.

The Libraries regularly displays materials from the Special Collections in its public Exhibition Gallery, located just outside the Dibner Library in the National Museum of American History.

The text of the guide was prepared by Ellen B. Wells, Head of the Special Collections Department from 1979 to 1994, and Leslie K. Overstreet, Reference Librarian in the Dibner Library. Nancy L. Matthews, Publications Officer, assisted in the organization of the booklet and the selection and editing of the material included. We acknowledge with gratitude the assistance of the Smithsonian Institution Press in publishing the guide.

Nancy E. Gwinn
Assistant Director
Collections Management
December 1994

"Baliste très orné . . . " [Very ornate trigger-fish]. Louis Isidore Duperrey. *Voyage autour du monde . . . sur . . . la Coquille* [Voyage around the world . . . on . . . the Coquille]. Paris, 1826–[38]. Vol. 5: *Histoire naturelle. Zoologie* [Natural history. Zoology], by René Primevère Lesson and Prosper Garnot.

This voyage of exploration was one of many that the French government sponsored in the late 1700s and early 1800s; all included naturalists who collected plant and animal specimens. The Ship's Surgeon Prosper Garnot and Assistant Surgeon and Pharmacist René Primevère Lesson were among those who carried out these activities and who later named and described the different species.

1.

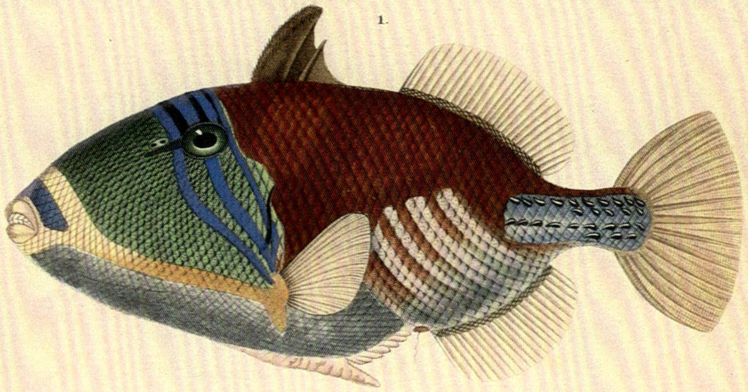

1/3

2.

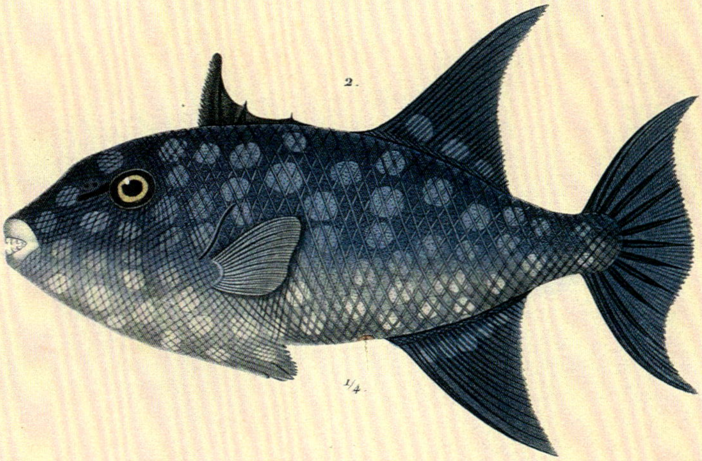

1/4

3.

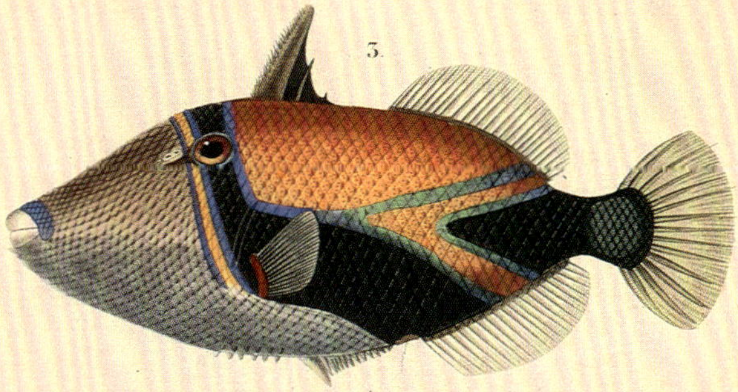

1/2

1. Baliste très orné. (Balistes ornatissimus, Less.)

2. Baliste azur. (Balistes azureus, Less.)

3. Baliste à pectorale bordée de rouge. (Balistes erythropteron, Less.)

Prêtre pinx.t d'après Lesson. *De l'imp.ie de Rémond.* *H. Legrand sculp.*

General Knowledge

REFERENCE WORKS PUBLISHED FROM THE FIFTEENTH CENTURY onward are invaluable guides for the research community. These encyclopedias, atlases, and dictionaries reflect the knowledge of the times and are the cornerstones of literacy and contemporary science. They also document the development of techniques, tools, and machinery.

The Libraries holds several early editions of Bartholomaeus Anglicus' *De proprietatibus rerum* [On the properties of things] (1230–50), a compilation of the world's religious and secular knowledge, including a manuscript dating from the late thirteenth century and an incunable printed in 1482, both from the Burndy Library donation.

Smithsonian researchers find many uses for the extensive collection of atlases and maps. The 1696 atlas from the Sanson family of cartographers brings together in an elegant fashion all the technical and artistic skills of mapmaking and printing of the time. George Wolworth Colton's nineteenth-century gazetteers provide obsolete place names useful to taxonomists for locating the sites where North American plants and animals were first found and described in the 1800s. They also indicate the territories inhabited by indigenous peoples before they were relocated.

Long runs of historical journals are a significant and wide-ranging resource in the Libraries' Special Collections. Especially rewarding are complete sets of the *Philosophical Transactions of the Royal Society of London,* which began publishing in 1665; *The Gentleman's Magazine,* 1731–1907; the *Annales des Ponts et Chausées* [Annals of bridges and roads], 1747–1815; and *The Universal Magazine,* 1747–1815. The *Description des arts et métiers* [Description of arts and crafts], 1761–81, was added in 1968 and is valued for its summaries of the sophisticated arts and crafts of Enlightenment Europe.

Over 40,000 volumes of scientific and technical journals, dating from the 1600s to the 1900s, were transferred to the Smithsonian Libraries in 1968 from the U.S. Patent Office Library. The earliest issues are housed in Special Collections, and the later publications are available in the National Museum of American History Branch Library.

Titus Lucretius Carus. *De rerum natura liber* [Book on the nature of things]. Verona, 1486. Gift of the Burndy Library.

This is the first dated edition of the scientific poem which set out Democritos' (460–370 B.C.) theory of atoms forming and reforming in the universe.

T. Lucreti Cari. poetæ philoſophici antiquiſſimi
de rerum natura liber primus incipit fœliciter.

AEneadū genitrix hominū diuūq; uoluptas
Alma uenus: cæli ſubter labentia ſigna
Quae mare nauigerum quae
terras frugiferentis
Concelebras: per te quoniam genus omne animantum
Concipitur. uiſitq; exortum lumina ſolis.
Te dea te fugiunt uenti: te nubila cæli
Aduentumq; tuum: tibi ſuauis dædala tellus
Submittit flores: tibi rident equora ponti.
Placatumq; nitet diffuſo numine cælum.
Nam ſimulas ſpeties patefacta eſt uerna diei
Et reſerata uiget genitalis aura fauoni
Aeriæ primum uolucres te diua tuumq;
Significant nutum: perculſe corda tua ui
Inde fere pecudes perſultans pabula læta
Et rapidos tranant aranis: ita capta lepore.
Te ſequitur cupide quocunq; inducere pergis.
Deniq; per maria ac montis flouioſq; rapacis
Frondiferaſq; domos auium: campoſq; uirentis
Omnibus incutiens blandum per pectora amorem
Efficis: ut cupide generatim ſæcla propagent.
Quae quoniam rerum naturam ſola gubernas:
Nec ſine te quicq̄ dias in luminis oras
Exoritur: neq; fit lætum: neq; amabile quicq̄.
Te ſotiam ſtudio ſcribendis uerſibus eſſe.
Quos ego de rerum natura pangere conor
Meminiadæ noſtro. quem tu dea tempore in omni
Omnibus ornatum noluiſti excellere rebus.
Quo magis æternum da dictis diua leporem
Effice: ut interea fera monera militiai
Per maria ac terras omnis ſopita quieſcant.
Nam tu ſola potes tranquilla pace iuuare
Mortalis. quoniam bellifera munera mauors
Armipotens regit. ingremium qui ſæpe tuum ſe
Reſicit. æterno deuictus uulnere amoris.
Atq; ira ſuſpiciens cereti ceruice repoſta
Paſcit amore auidos inhians in te dea uiſus.
Atq; tuo pendet reſupini ſpiritus ore.

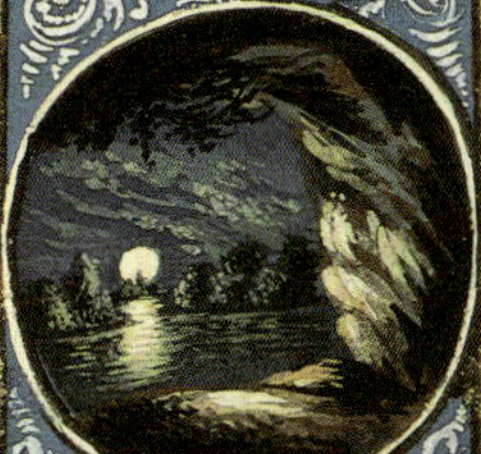

a ii

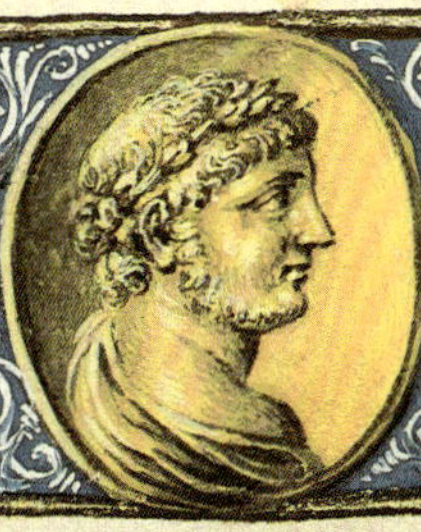

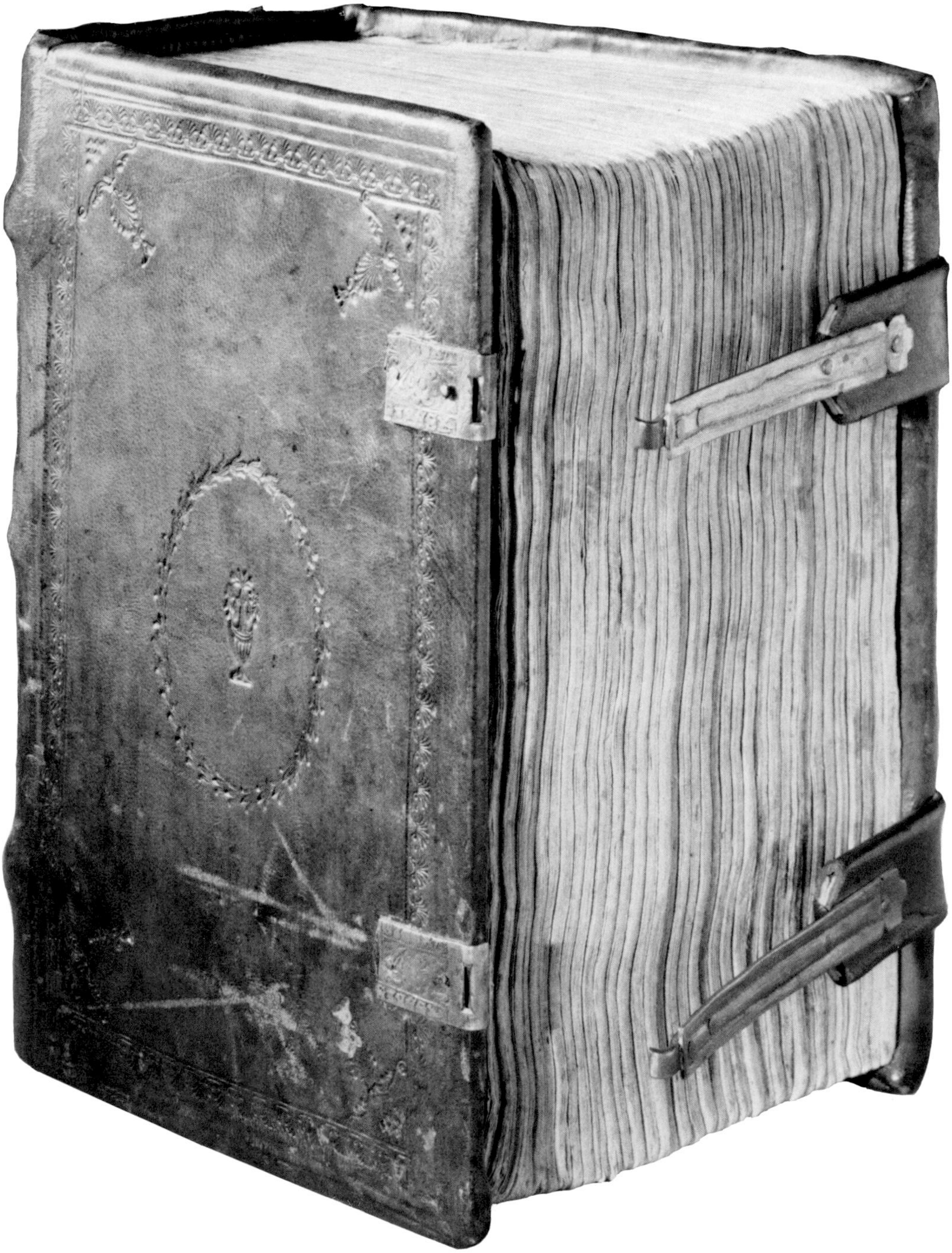

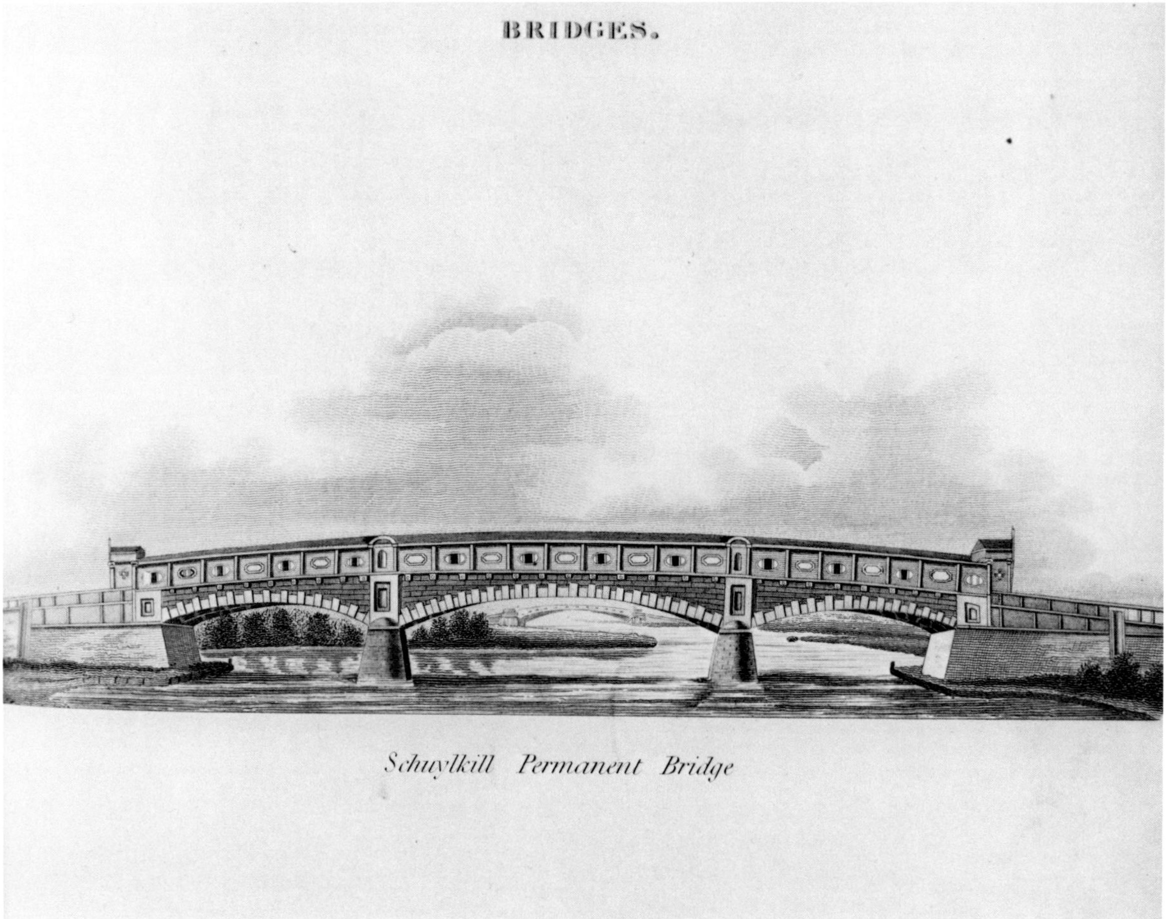

Above: "Schuylkill Permanent Bridge." Abraham Rees. *Cyclopædia; or, universal dictionary of arts, sciences, and literature.* Philadelphia, 1802–20.

The first United States edition of an older British encyclopedia was "enlarged and adapted to this country" with references to American objects and events. The Cyclopædia, *in 47 volumes, recorded existing technology in great detail.*

Opposite: Johann Stoeffler. *Almanach nova in annos 1499–1531* [New almanac for the years 1499–1531]. [Ulm, 1499.] Gift of the Burndy Library.

This encyclopedic compilation is encased in an eighteenth-century leather binding.

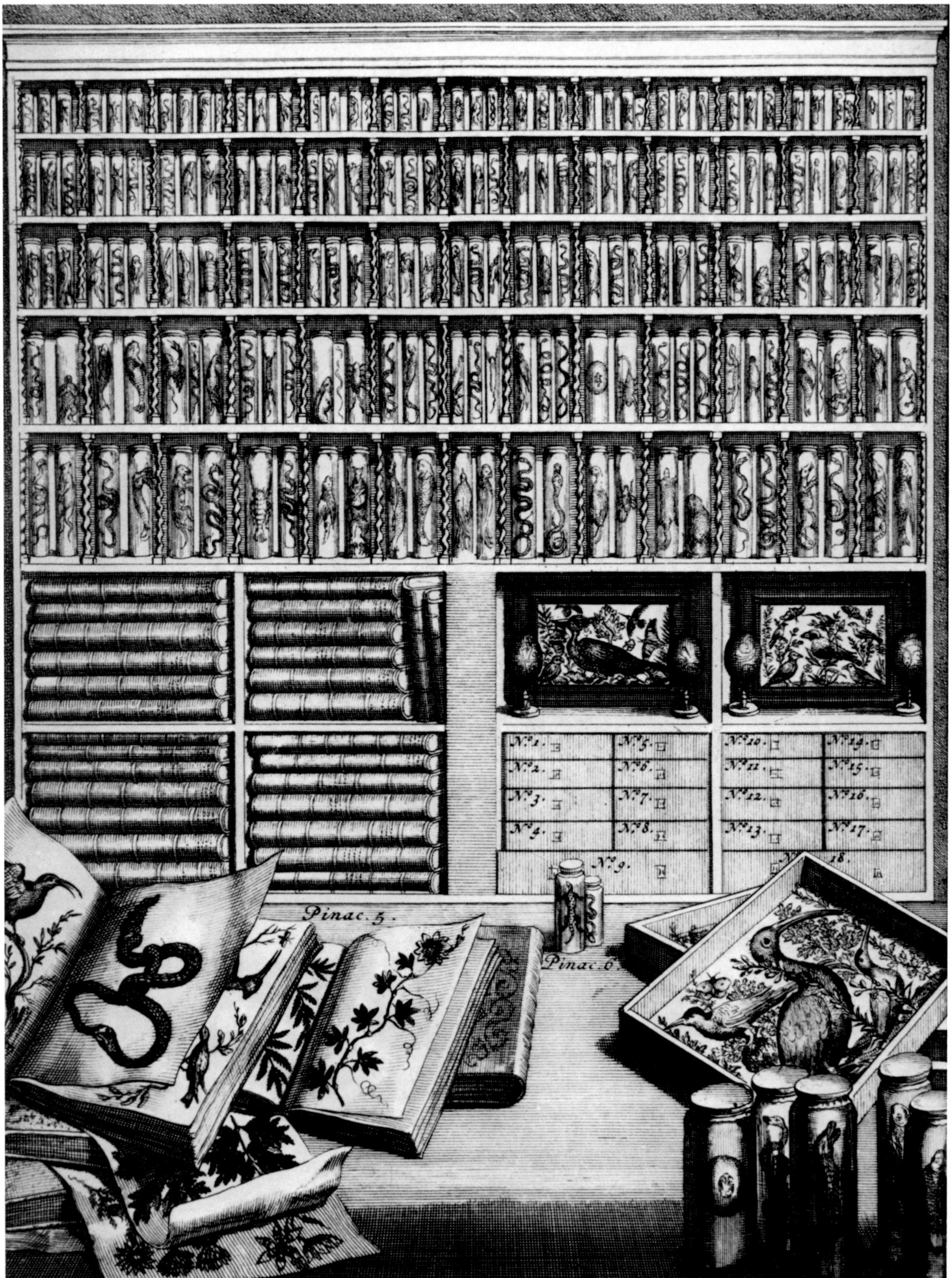
N°1.
N°5.
N°10.
N°14.
N°2.
N°6.
N°11.
N°15.
N°3.
N°7.
N°12.
N°16.
N°4.
N°8.
N°13.
N°17.
N°9.
18
Pinac. 5.
Pinac. 6.

Museums

SITUATED IN THE MIDST OF THE LARGEST MUSEUM COMPLEX IN THE world, the Libraries' Special Collections have exceptional holdings in the history of museums, collecting of specimens, and conservation of materials.

Levinus Vincent. *Elenchus tabularum . . . in gazophylacio Levini Vincent* [A series of illustrations . . . of the collection of the wonders of nature of Levin Vincent]. Haarlem, The Netherlands, 1719.

This book describes the private "cabinet" collection of Levin Vincent, a Dutch merchant (1658–1727). The illustration shows animal specimens preserved in alcohol in glass jars, plant specimens dried and pressed on large sheets of paper, and volumes of illustrations of plants and animals. These categories of materials, together with skeletons and skins (both feathers and fur), remain the core of today's natural history collections.

Early Science Museums

The progenitors of today's museums are the private "cabinets of rarities" and "wonder rooms" of earlier centuries, many of which are described in Renaissance works housed in the collections.

Natural history collections and the manuscripts and printed books describing them became scientifically significant in the 1600s. The best of them were serious, systematic efforts to investigate and comprehend the natural world. From the seventeenth century on, such efforts were greatly expanded as scientific expeditions sponsored by royalty and merchants brought exotic plants and animals back to European collections. Some of these collections developed considerably and, by the late 1700s, formed the foundations of modern national, provincial, and university museum collections.

The books written by scientific collectors and classifiers from the sixteenth through the eighteenth centuries are the core of the Libraries' resources on museum history. These include Ferrante Imperato's *Dell'historia naturale* [*On natural history*] (Naples, 1599), Ole Worm's *Museum Wormianum* [The Wormian museum] (Leyden, 1655), and the works of Ulisse Aldrovandi, published between the 1590s and 1640s, many posthumously. Special Collections also holds later publications that catalog the collections of the established museums, carrying their histories forward into the nineteenth century and the modern period.

Technological and cultural collections in Renaissance Europe emphasized mechanical devices, like intricate clockworks and automata, and scientific instruments, such as astrolabes and telescopes. This fascination with the beauty, wonder, and power of human craftsmanship and ingenuity continued into the nineteenth century, and is expressed by the enthusiasm for world's fairs and national expositions displaying the industrial and decorative arts. The Libraries' holdings in this field begin with Pierre Borel's *Antiquitez, raretez . . . de la ville & comte de Castres d'Albigeois* [The antiquities, rarities . . . of the city and Count of Castres of Albigeois] (Castres, 1649) and Holger Jacobaeus' *Museum regium; seu, Catalogus rerum tam naturalium, quam artificialium* [The royal museum; or, A catalog of things both natural and artificial] (Copenhagen, 1696), as well as Athanasius Kircher's *Musæum Kircherianum* [The Kircherian museum] (Rome, 1709). A strong collection on world's fairs and expositions from the 1840s to 1916 provides a wealth of primary material for studies in a variety of fields.

"Ammonshorn" (*Nautilus umbilicatus*). Georg Wolfgang Knorr. *Vernugen der Augen und des Gemuths* [Delights for the eyes and senses]. Nuremberg, 1757–72.

A distinguished book in the long history of malacology (or conchology), Knorr's work illustrates a variety of exotic shells, many of which, like this one, were specimens in private European collections.

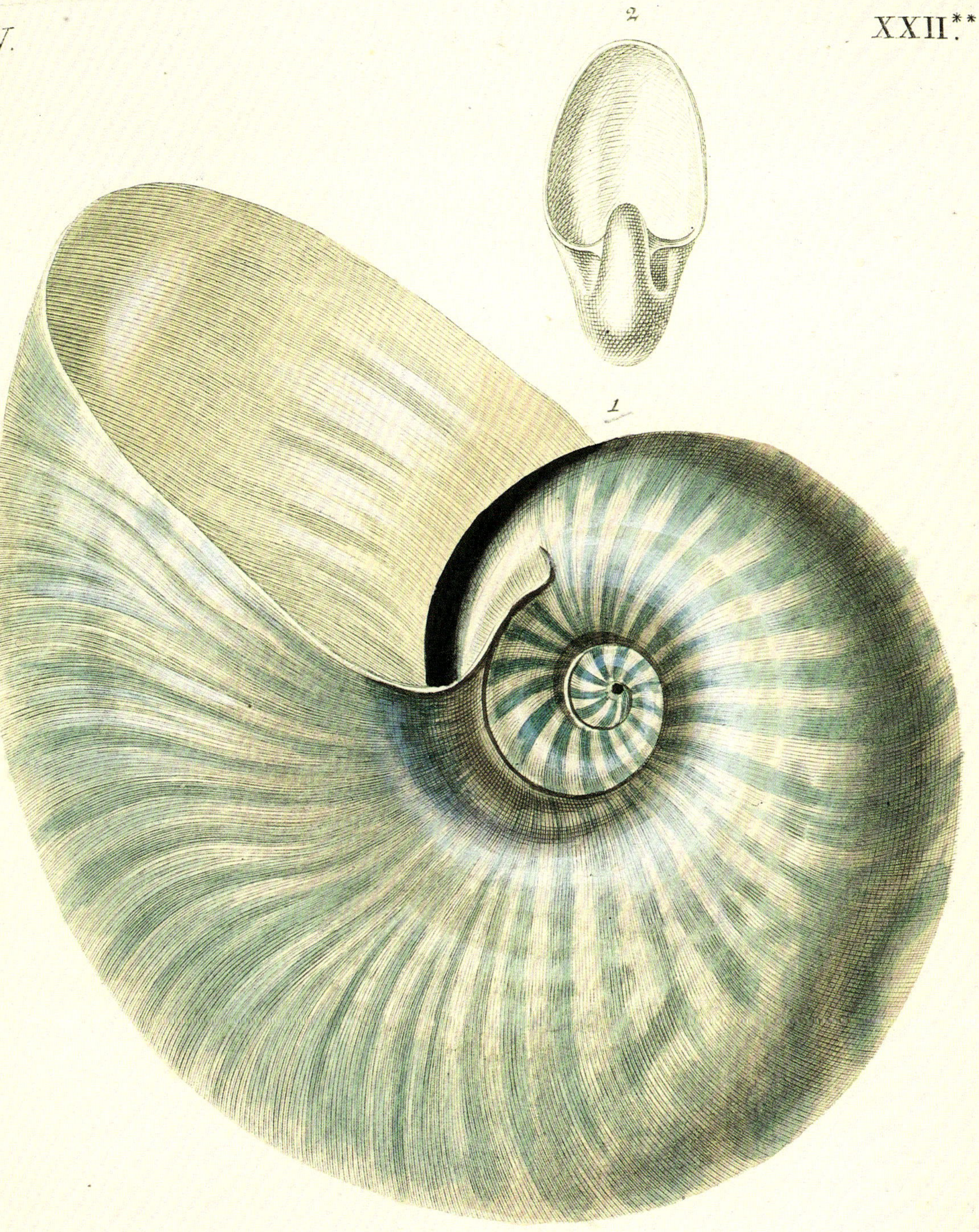

Ex Museo Schadeloockiano.

J.C. Keller ad nat. pinxit. Andr. Hoffer sculps.

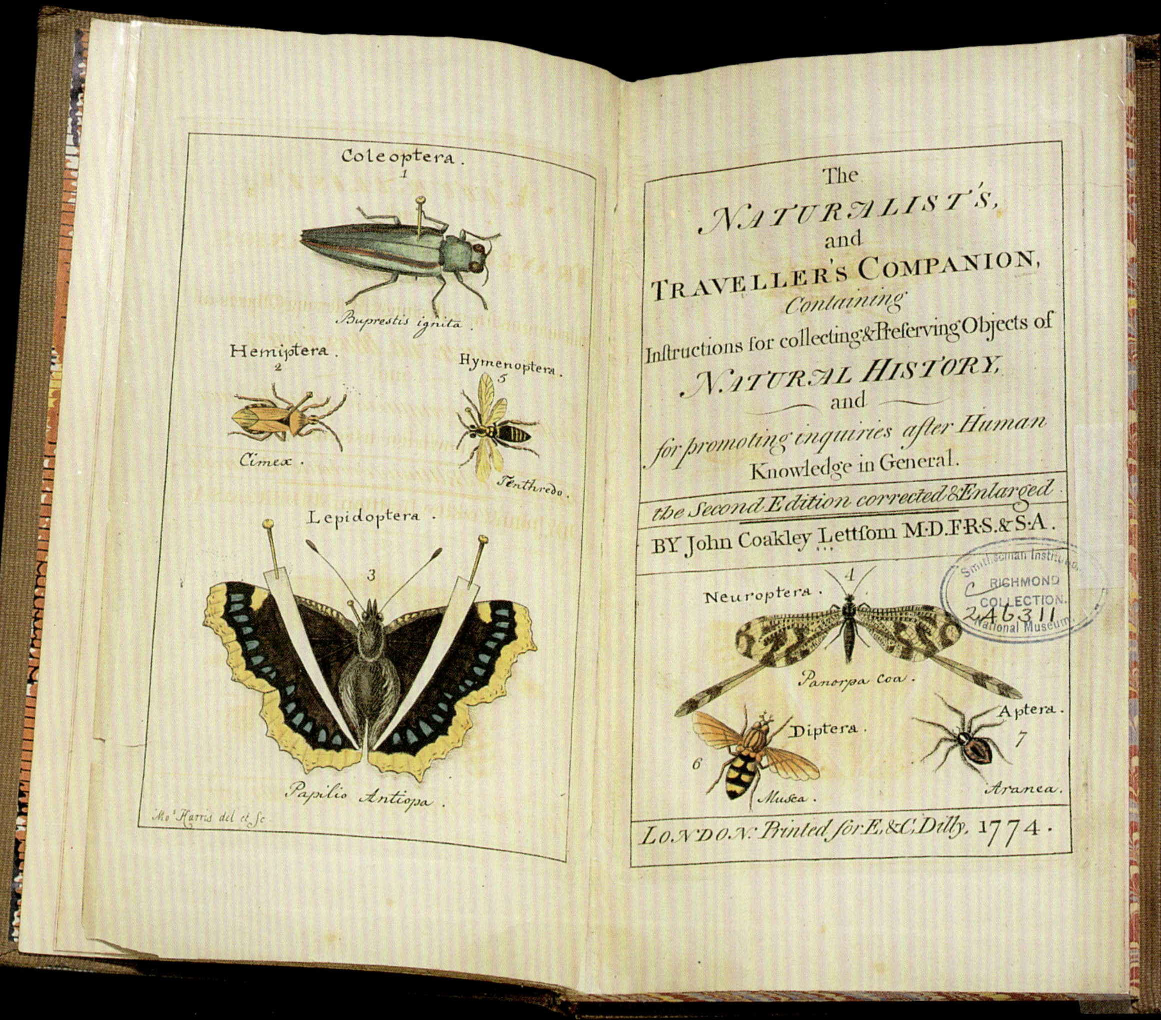
Coleoptera.
1
Buprestis ignita.
Hemiptera.
2
Cimex.
Hymenoptera.
5
Tenthredo.
Lepidoptera.
3
Papilio Antiopa.
Mo. Harris del et Sc
The
NATURALIST'S,
and
TRAVELLER'S COMPANION,
Containing
Instructions for collecting & Preserving Objects of
NATURAL HISTORY,
and
for promoting inquiries after Human
Knowledge in General.
the Second Edition corrected & Enlarged
BY John Coakley Lettsom M.D. F.R.S. & S.A.
Neuroptera.
4
Panorpa Coa.
Diptera.
6
Musca.
Aptera.
7
Aranea.
LONDON: Printed for E. & C. Dilly, 1774.
Smithsonian Institution
RICHMOND
COLLECTION.
246311
National Museum.

Scientific Collecting and Conservation

Collectors' field guides and manuals for preparing specimens for storage and exhibition are crucial collateral publications relating to and supporting research in the formation and preservation of collections. A bequest from Alexander Wetmore, the Smithsonian's sixth Secretary (1945–52) and a distinguished ornithologist, added depth to the Libraries' collection of collectors' and conservators' manuals in the natural sciences.

In the technological and cultural collections, books and manuscripts from the seventeenth through the nineteenth centuries support research on the original construction and manufacture of objects, on finishes and decoration, and on restoration and preservation. Practical matters like design sources, construction diagrams, trade recipes, and formulas for lacquers and paints are addressed throughout. In 1990 the Libraries purchased the Robert D. Mussey, Jr., collection on varnishes, a rich resource of old craft manuals and trade catalogs—many of them extremely rare. This collection includes Robert Dossie's *Handmaid to the arts* (1764), Andreas Zeidler's *Neu-entdecket lacquir-kunst* [Newly discovered lacquer arts] (1797), and Jean Felix Watin's *L'art du peintre, doreur, vernisseur* [The art of the painter, gilder, (and) varnisher] (1776).

John Coakley Lettsom. *The naturalist's and traveller's companion, containing instructions for collecting & preserving objects of natural history.* 2nd edition, corrected and enlarged. London, 1774. From the Charles W. Richmond collection.

Born in the West Indies to British Quaker parents, Lettsom (1744–1815) migrated to England and became a physician with a thriving medical practice. He also collected specimens for his own private natural-history museum and botanical garden, and conducted a vast correspondence with the leading naturalists of his day, including Linnaeus (Carl von Linné, the eighteenth-century Swedish botanist and zoologist). Lettsom's manual, one of the earliest and fullest accounts of collecting methods and materials, was first published by the author in 1772, and its success led to further editions.

This copy of the second edition was acquired by Charles W. Richmond, a Smithsonian ornithologist in the early twentieth century. Practical manuals such as this one which shed light on collecting practices are of particular interest to Smithsonian staff who now study the Institution's natural history collections. The Libraries also holds a copy of the third edition (1799), received by bequest from Alexander Wetmore, ornithologist and Secretary of the Institution.

Smithsoniana

The Libraries' *Smithsoniana* collection contains the Institution's official publications as well as works about the Institution, including sets of the annual reports, proceedings and bulletins dating from the Smithsonian's U.S. National Museum, and other early Smithsonian publications. Publications relating to the Institution's establishment, together with a variety of early guides to its buildings and collections, are of special interest. These printed materials supplement the manuscript material and internal records available in the Smithsonian Institution Archives.

Ernest Ingersoll. *Handbook to the National Museum*. New York, 1886.

Within thirty years of the founding of the Smithsonian and the construction of the Castle, where its collections were housed and displayed, it was clear that more space was needed. In 1881 a building was added next to the Castle and designated the U.S. National Museum; it is now known as the Arts and Industries Building. This handbook was the first guide to the new museum's exhibits, research collections, and facilities.

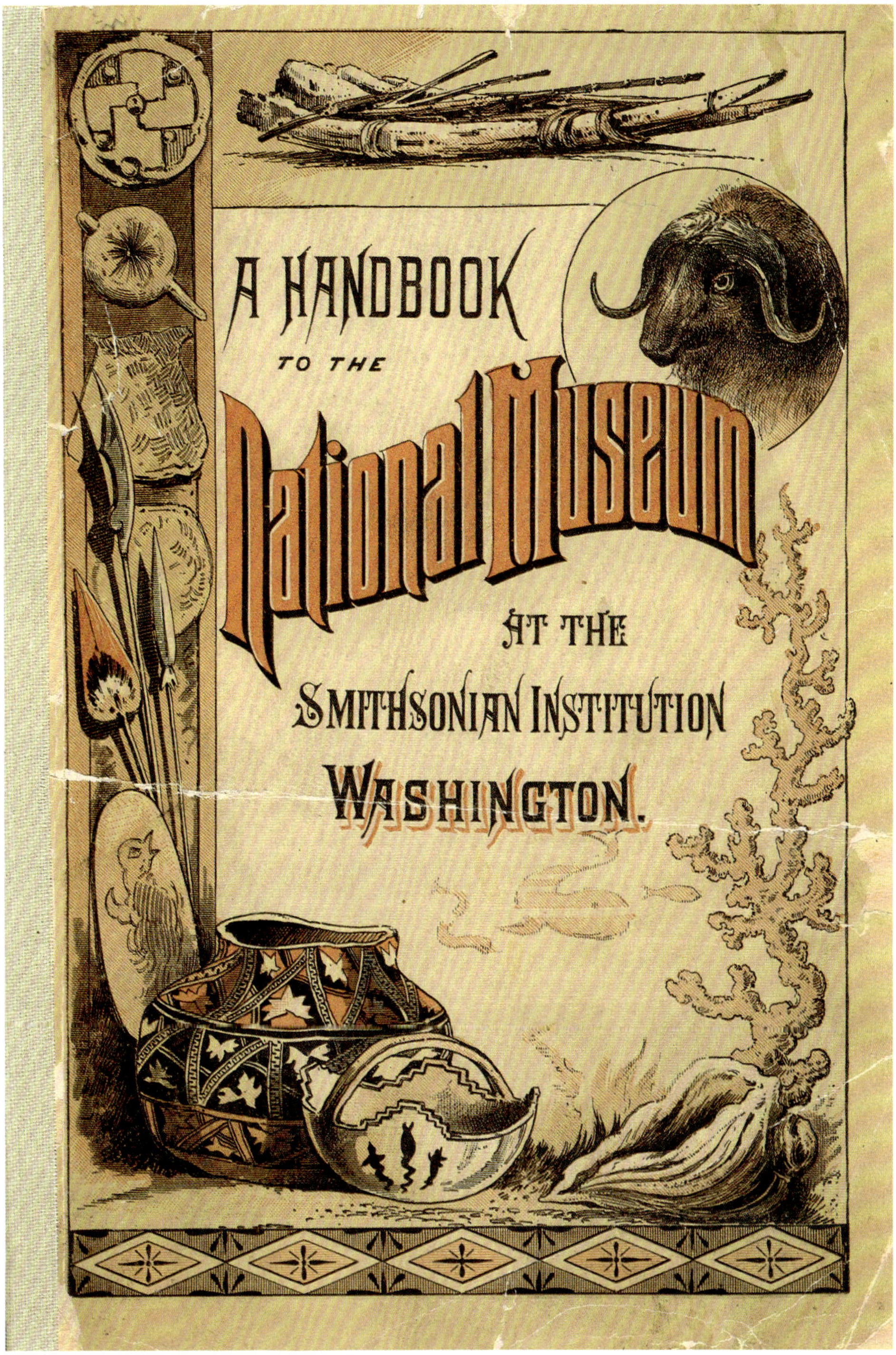
A HANDBOOK
TO THE
National Museum
AT THE
SMITHSONIAN INSTITUTION
WASHINGTON.

yellow and red; pale blue, pale red. The Diameter of the second Crown measured from the middle of the yellow and red on one side of the Sun, to the middle of the same Colour on the other side was 9¼ Degrees, or thereabouts. The Diameters of the first and third I had not time to measure, but that of the first seemed to be about five or six Degrees, and that of the third about twelve. The like Crowns appear sometimes about the Moon; for in the beginning of the Year 1664, *Febr.* 19th at Night, I saw two such Crowns about her. The Diameter of the first or innermost was about three Degrees, and that of the second about five Degrees and an half. Next about the Moon was a Circle of white, and next about that the inner Crown, which was of a bluish green within next the white, and of a yellow and red without, and next about these Colours were blue and green on the inside of the outward Crown, and red on the outside of it. At the same time there appear'd a Halo about 22 Degrees 35′ distant from the center of the Moon. It was elliptical, and its long Diameter was perpendicular to the Horizon, verging below farthest from the Moon. I am told that the Moon has sometimes three or more concentrick Crowns of Colours encompassing one another next about her Body. The more equal the globules of Water or Ice are to one another, the more Crowns of Colours will appear, and the Colours will be the more lively. The Halo at the distance of 22½ Degrees from the

x I saw the like appearance.

Jan. 1. 1729-30 at 8h p.m.

The moon was near the full & shone through a white cloud which made her spots appear invisible. I judged the semidiameter of ye white cloud to contain 5 or 6 of the moons diameters. It was very white next the moon ... gradually tinged with yellow which grew stronger & made a yellow ring; next about it was a ring of orange and next about these was a ring of dull dirty or dusky blue & next about it a ring of green; the bredth of the two last rings together was about a degree; and they were encompassed with a ring of yellow & this with a ring of orange. The air was very clear & sharp & the sky was interspersed with white clouds like that which the moon shone through, which was blown over the moon in half a minute & put an end to the appear

The Rings were not exactly round, but concentric to the moon.

p. 174

See p. 181 obs. 9. p. 207

p. 186 obs. 15.

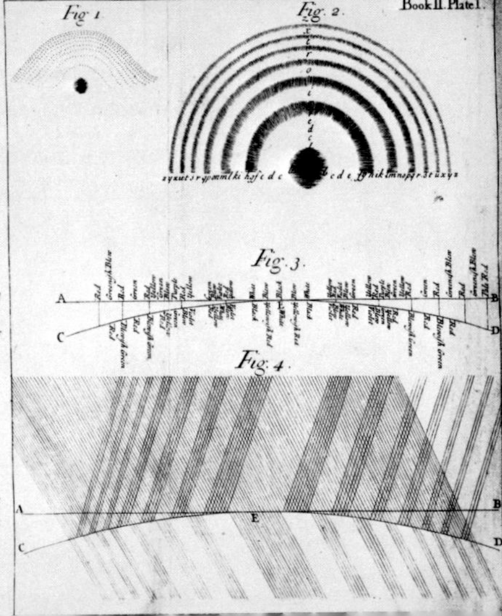

Physical Sciences and Mathematics

THE BURNDY LIBRARY DONATION GREATLY ENRICHED SPECIAL Collections resources in mathematics and the physical sciences—especially physics, chemistry, earth sciences, astronomy, and related works on measurement and instrumentation. In addition to printed works, the gift included some 1,600 manuscript groups reflecting over 500 years of scientific and technological development, mostly in the physical sciences. Among these are a dozen alchemical manuscripts of Isaac Newton and miscellaneous correspondence of the abbé Jean Antoine Nollet, Felix Ehrenhaft, John Tyndall, and many other figures associated with early science and research. Manuscript versions of works on natural philosophy, including Aristotle's *Physica* and the *Sphæra* of Johannes de Sacro Bosco, add value to the collections.

Seventeenth- and eighteenth-century lecture notes, well represented in the manuscript collections, provide firsthand records of early scientific education and the growth of scientific knowledge. Examples are two volumes on natural philosophy written in 1774 by H. Kok and a 300-page *Notes on a course of lectures on chemistry delivered by Mr. [William Thomas] Brande in the laboratory of the Royal Institution in 1819*, penned by an unknown student. Some student notes have engraved plates bound with them showing experiments and mechanical models.

Isaac Newton. *Opticks; or, A treatise of the reflections, refractions, inflections and colours of light.* London, 1718. Gift of the Burndy Library.

The Libraries has many editions and several translations of Newton's publications, some with interesting provenance. The owner-annotator of this copy of the Opticks *was Newton's younger contemporary, Robert Smith, a Cambridge University professor and author of the most influential textbook on optics in the eighteenth century. The engraved illustration was printed on a sheet cut blank on the left, and mounted on a wide tab to permit the plate to be seen at the same time as the relevant text. Smith wrote his comments on the blank sheet provided.*

Mathematics

The history of mathematics can be followed in groups of works produced by a number of illustrious scientific families. Several generations of the Bernoullis of Switzerland specialized in mathematics and physics; among them, Daniel Bernoulli was responsible for the principle bearing his name concerning the properties of gases. The Hungarian Bolyais, father and son, published mathematical works that are now extremely rare. Four generations of the Italian-French Cassini family were astronomers and directors of the Observatory of Paris; their works detail numerous advances and discoveries in astronomy. In addition, the Dibner Library holds over forty different publications of the prodigiously inventive mathematician Leonhard Euler.

"To inscribe a circle in a given square." Euclid. *The first six books of the elements of Euclid.* [Edited] by Oliver Byrne. London, 1847. Gift of the Burndy Library.

Oliver Byrne believed that students would learn more easily and quickly if color was used to emphasize Euclid's geometry theories. Publisher William Pickering produced this beautifully printed edition with an extravagance of color.

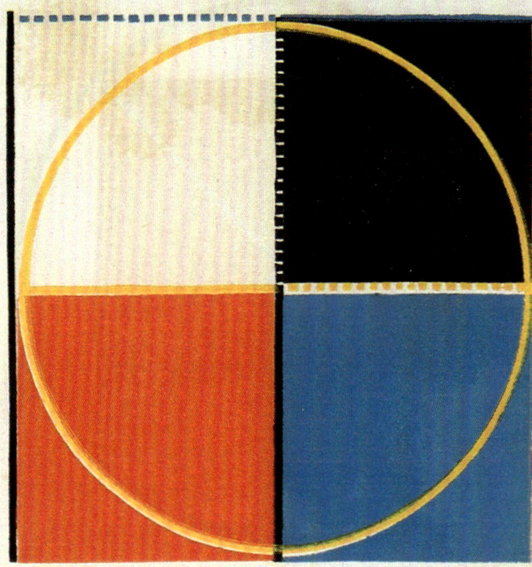

TO inscribe a circle in a given square.

Make = ,

and = ,

draw || ,

and || 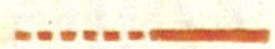

(B. 1. pr. 31.)

∴  is a parallelogram;

and since = (hyp.)

 =

∴  is equilateral (B. 1. pr. 34.)

In like manner, it can be shown that

 =  are equilateral parallelograms;

∴ = = = 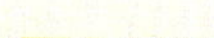 ,

and therefore if a circle be described from the concourse of these lines with any one of them as radius, it will be inscribed in the given square. (B. 3. pr. 16.)

Q. E. D.

Mapping the Earth and Heavens

As more information on the continents and geography of the world was discovered and recorded, maps became more reliable. The improvement of surveying and astronomical instruments like the astrolabe, and later the telescope and marine chronometer, enabled astronomers, navigators, and geographers to create ever more detailed maps of the earth and to describe an increasing number of known stars and other celestial bodies. From the writings of Galileo Galilei to those of William Herschel and his sister and collaborator, Caroline Lucretia Herschel, Special Collections houses impressive research classics.

Johannes Hevelius. *Machinæ cœlestis* [Celestial machines, or astronomical instruments]. Danzig, 1673–79. Gift of the Burndy Library.

In this work Hevelius, a German astronomer and instrument-maker, describes the observatory he built. Hevelius is shown here with his wife on the roof with one of his open-sight quadrants. His observatory is reported as the best equipped in Europe and included a workshop for making instruments.

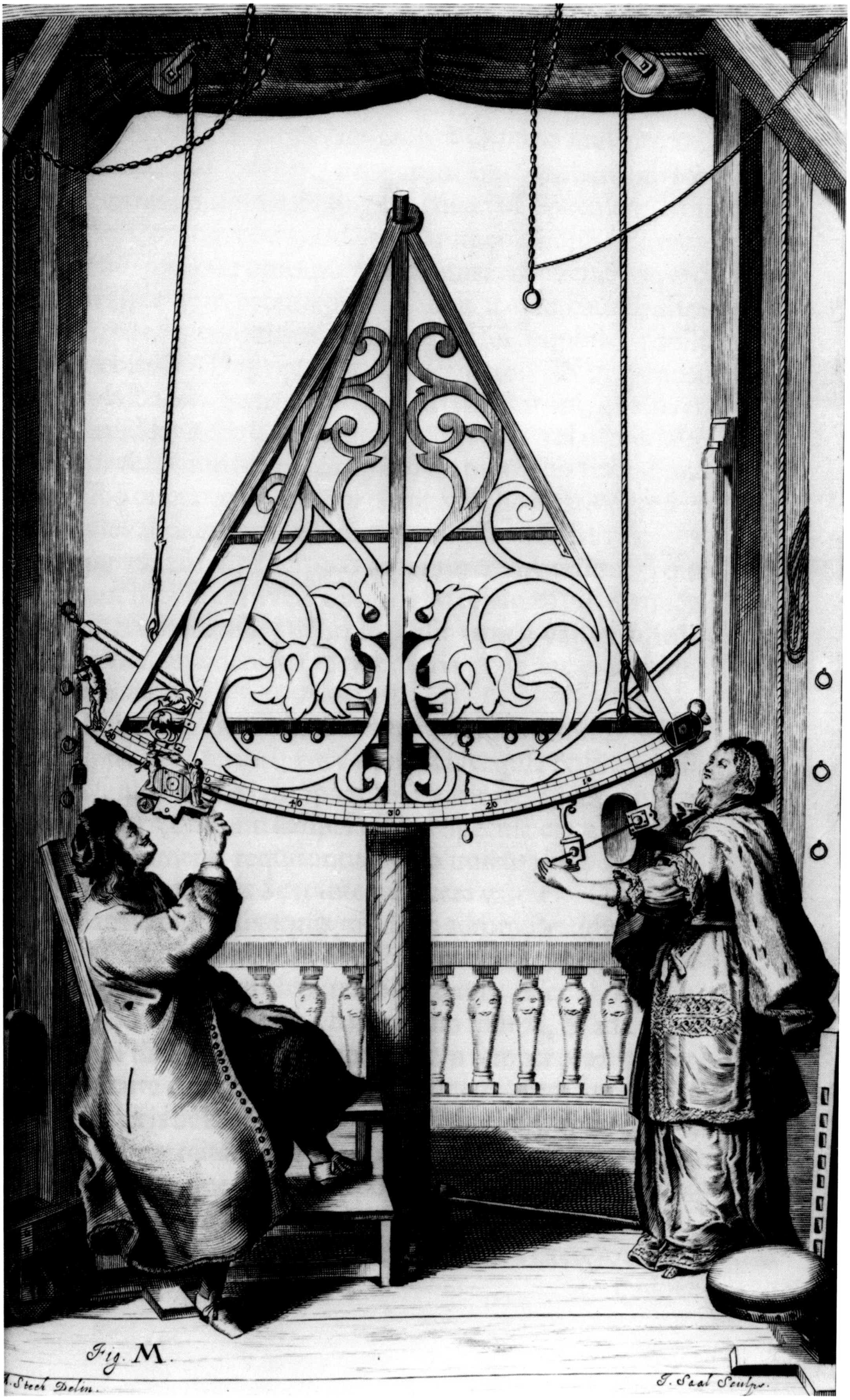

30
40
20
10
Fig. M.
A. Steech Delin.
J. Saal Sculps.

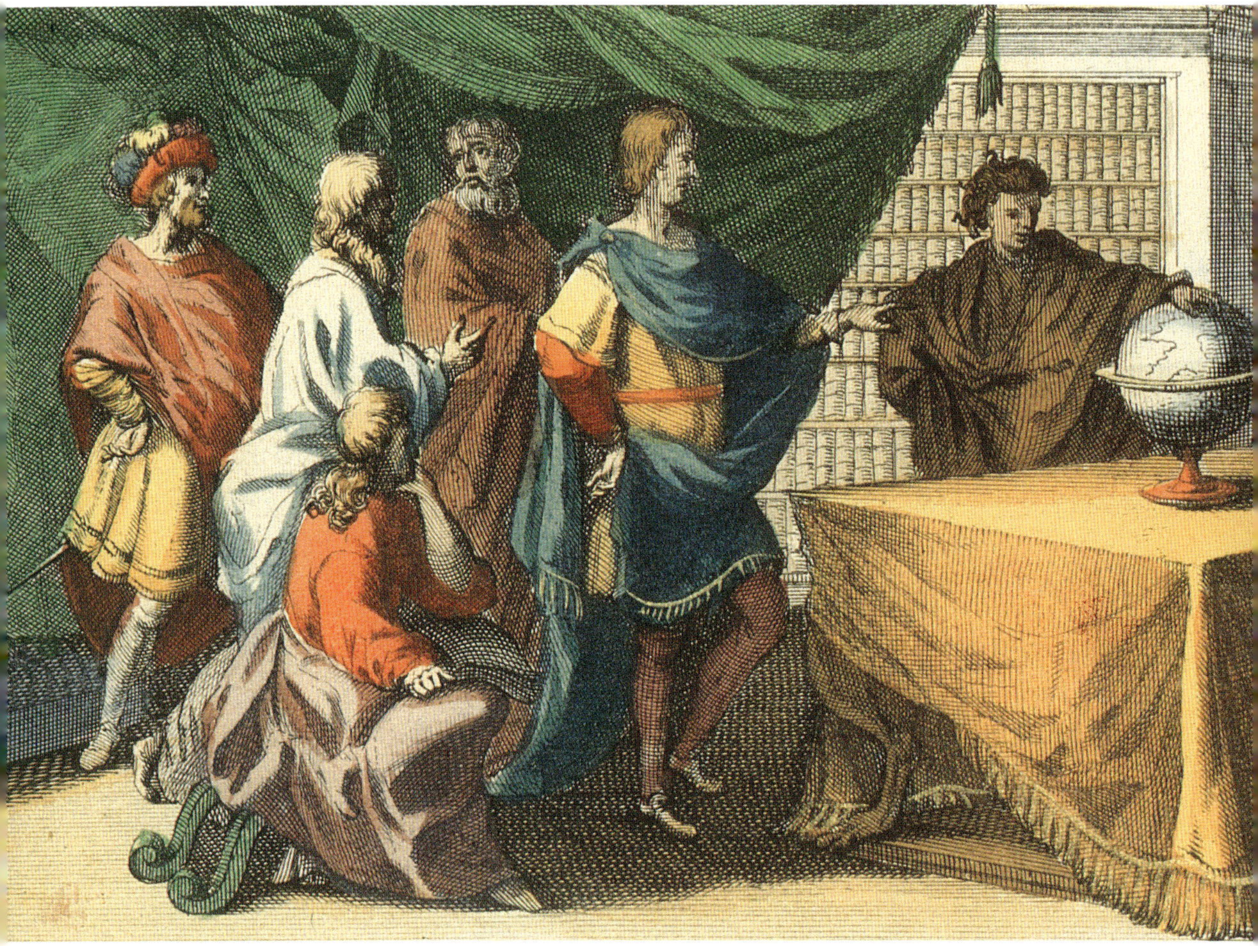

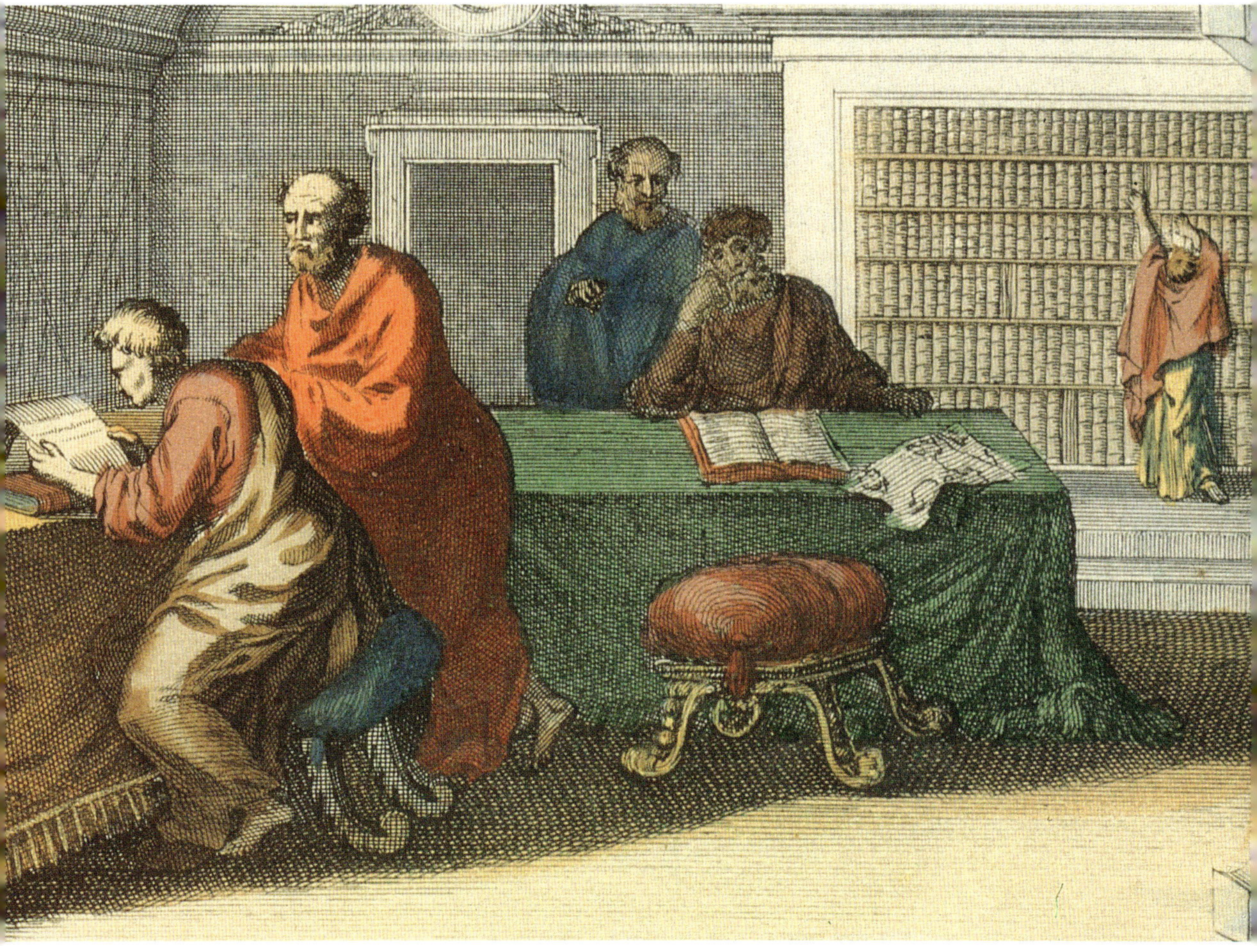

"Tables des cartes" [List of maps] (detail). Nicolas Sanson. *Atlas nouveau, contenant toutes les parties du monde* [A new atlas, containing all the parts of the world]. Paris, [1692?].

Sanson, head of a distinguished family of mapmakers, was responsible for establishing the great French school of cartography. His atlas divided the world into four parts—Europe, Africa, Asia, and America—and his maps are known for their clear graphics, especially the fine lettering and careful spacing of details.

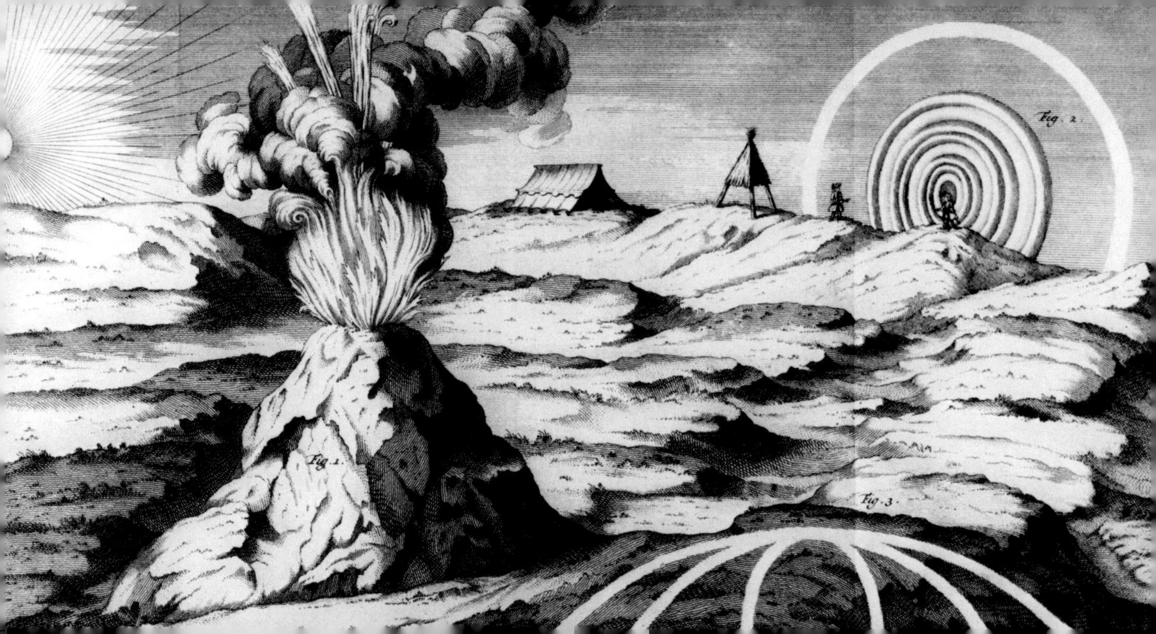
Fig. 1.
Fig. 2.
Fig. 3.

Earth Sciences

IN THE EARTH SCIENCES THE SPECIAL COLLECTIONS SERVES Smithsonian staff and other researchers in a variety of disciplines, including scientists who classify minerals by microscopic analyses of crystal structure, paleontologists and biodiversity specialists concerned with the deposit and distribution of fossil species, and volcanologists investigating the earth's seismic history.

"Montagne de Cotopaxi" [Cotopaxi Mountain]. Antonio de Ulloa. *Voyage historique de l'Amerique meridionale* [Historic voyage to southern America]. Amsterdam and Leipzig, 1752.

The Spanish naval officer Antonio de Ulloa y de la Torre Giral accompanied Charles-Marie de La Condamine on an expedition to the Americas to measure an arc of meridian. His account of the expedition, sponsored by the Paris Académie des Sciences, includes descriptions of the volcanic eruptions of Cotopaxi and other active volcanoes in Ecuador as well as the first scientific description of the platinum deposits in Colombia.

Geology and Minerals

The Burndy Library donation brought to Special Collections the writings of many classical and medieval natural philosophers—Aristotle, Theophrastus, Strabo, Pliny, Avicenna, and Albertus Magnus among them—who speculated about the origin and nature of the physical world and the forces that form and change it. The donation also included, in many editions and translations, the key works of Agricola (Georg Bauer of Saxony, 1494–1555), whose pioneering works on mining and metals earned him the title of father of mineralogy and metallurgy. From his experiences as the elected town physician of a major mining center in eastern Europe, he described occupational diseases caused by exposure to metals in his *De re metallica* [On mining, ore processing, and metallurgy] (1557), his chief work, compiled over a period of twenty years.

Special Collections has extensive holdings of materials by eighteenth- and nineteenth-century authors Axel Frederik Cronstedt, Abraham Gottlob Werner, Charles Lyell, Sir Robert Impey Murchison, and many others whose works document the earth sciences as they began to coalesce into a distinct field. The study of geological forces and the differentiation of minerals was well under way by the mid-nineteenth century, and the term geology assumed its modern meaning, the study of the earth's history.

Of particular interest to museum researchers is the long controversy on how to classify minerals: by external characteristics or by internal structure. The internalists ultimately prevailed. Among those engaged in this debate whose works are represented in Special Collections are René-Just Haüy, Jean-Baptiste Louis de Romé de l'Isle, and Alexandre Brongniart.

Adolf Kenngott. *Illustrierte mineralogie* [Mineralogy illustrated]. 4th ed. Esslingen, [1888?].

This book on the natural history of plants, animals, and minerals appeared in a German series intended for students; it is the first of two volumes on minerals (the second covered geology and paleontology), and presents minerals in a classified system based on their crystal structure and chemical composition.

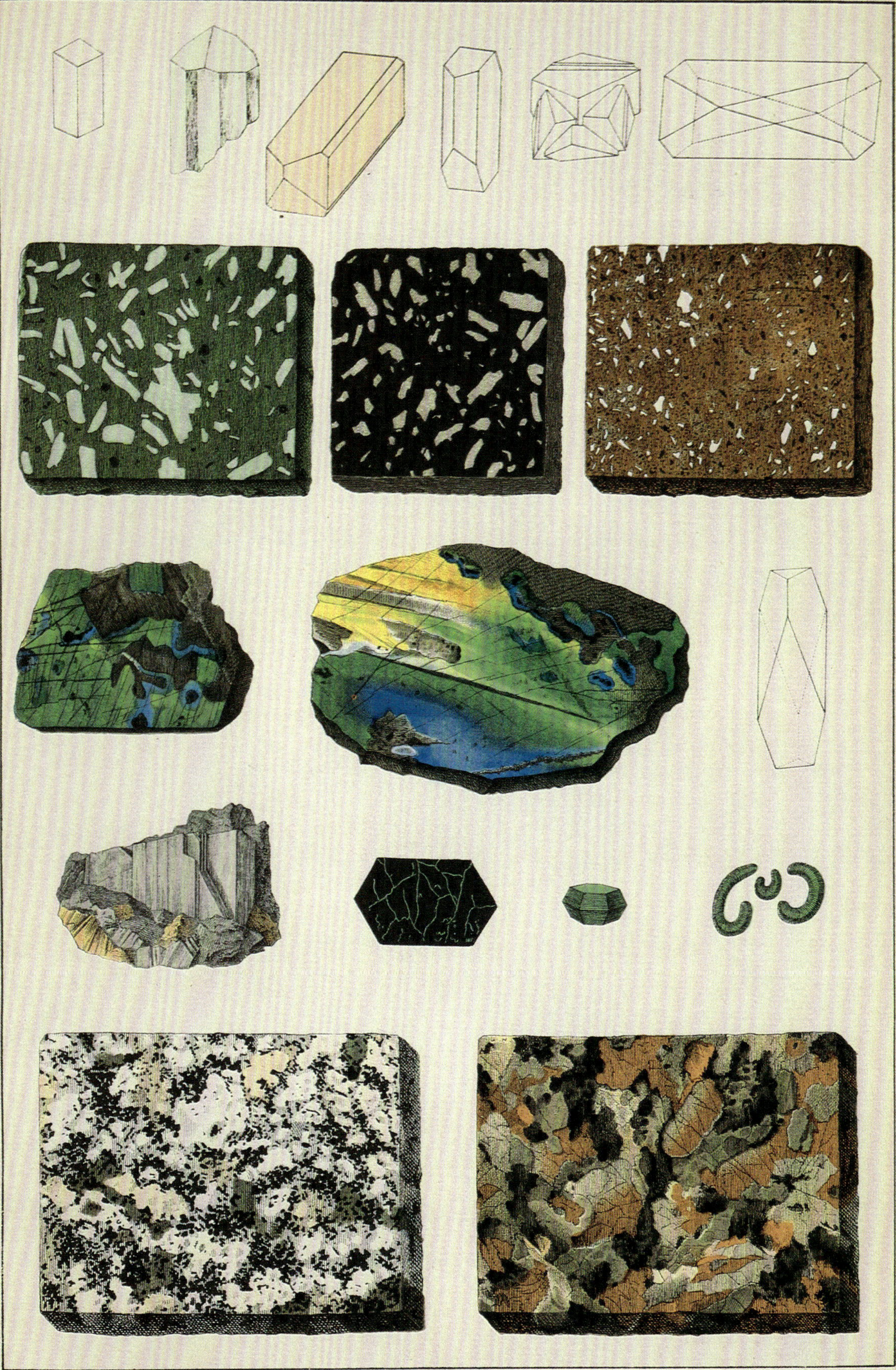

Paleontology

Technically a biological science, paleontology is inseparably tied to the study of geology, since the presence and identity of fossils are linked to geological strata and the processes which form topographical features. In organizing fossils in their "mineral" and "metal" cabinet collections, Renaissance scholars like Ulisse Aldrovandi, Ferrante Imperato, Michele Mercati, and Konrad Gesner, whose works are held in Special Collections, fought their way clear of speculation, religious dogma, and folklore in their attempts to create systems of scientific classification. Titles like Gesner's *De omni rerum fossilium genere, gemmis, lapidibus, metallis, et huiusmodi* [On all kinds of fossils, gems, stones, metals, and such] (Zurich, 1565–66) are indicative of both the tangle and the emerging clarity of classification.

Thanks to the studies of Nicolas Steno, Johann Jakob Scheuchzer, and Robert Hooke in the late seventeenth century, fossils were finally identified and accepted as traces or remains of animals and plants that have been preserved in the earth's crust. Paleontological knowledge—most important, the recognition that fossils are associated with specific geological layers of the earth and that many fossils represent species now extinct—was thereafter advanced in the works of Georges Cuvier, William Smith, Jean Baptiste de Lamarck, and Adolphe Brongniart.

Darwin's theories in *On the origin of species* (London, 1859) contributed the deciding arguments to the long-standing controversy surrounding paleontological theories on evolution and extinctions and stimulated great popular interest. Special Collections' holdings of works by the authors mentioned here and by other scientists who made seminal contributions support the systematic classification of fossils, work carried on by Smithsonian scientists today.

"Molar tooth of Mastodon maximus." James Hall. *Geology of New York. Part IV.* Albany, 1843.

Part of the lengthy Natural history of New York, *published under the auspices of New York State's Natural History Survey, this volume is the fruit of Hall's great skill and vigor in collecting examples of the state's fine paleontological remains.*

173.

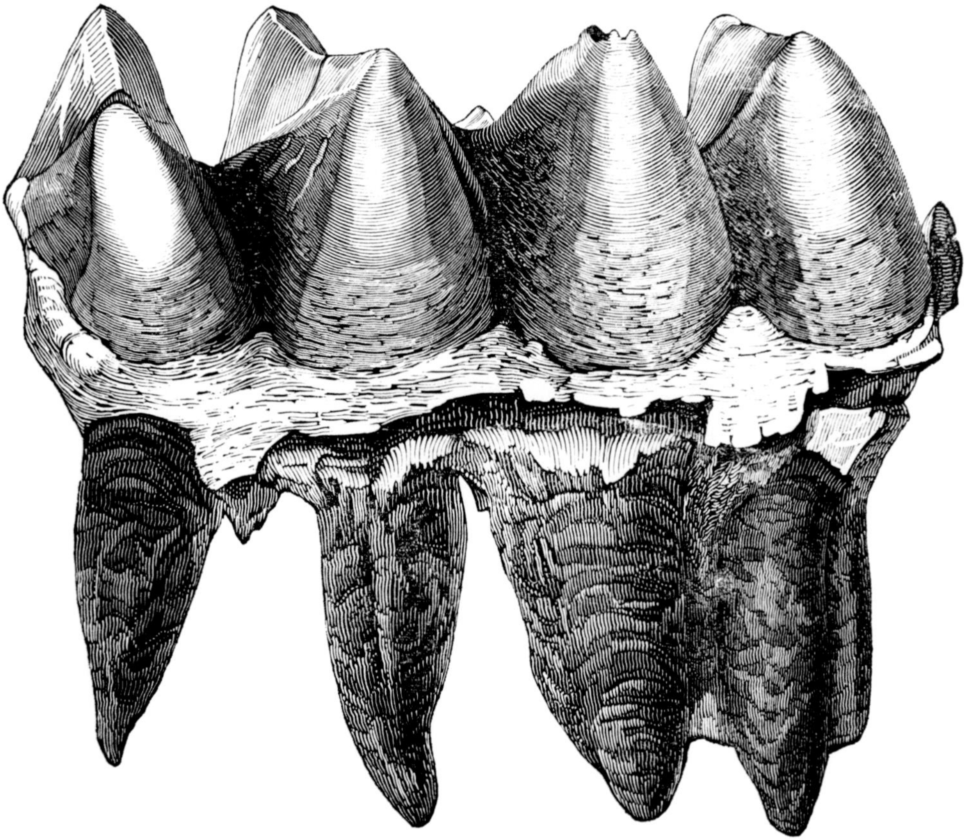

Molar tooth of Mastodon maximus. Genesco, Livingston county.

CHAPTER XVII.

Fossil Bones of Quadrupeds.

Fossil bones of the Mastodon have been found in numerous localities throughout the district, and, since the relative period of their existence is one of much interest, it seems desirable to ascertain the comparative date of the formation in which they are imbedded. These remains are not only distributed throughout the Fourth District, but have been found in all that part of the State west of the Hudson river and south of the valley of the Mohawk. But

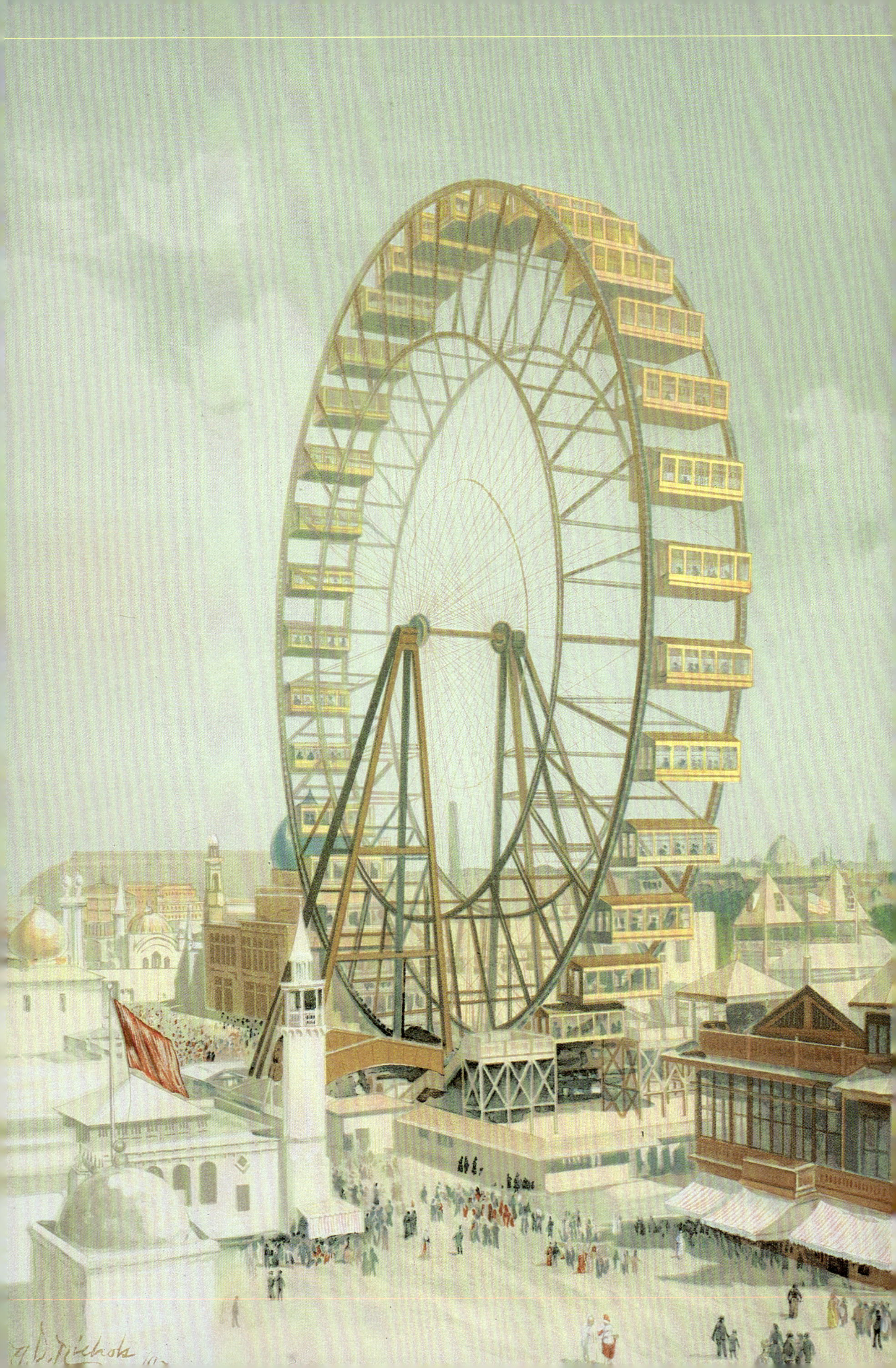

Technology, Industry, Engineering

THE LIBRARIES OFFERS EXCEPTIONAL OPPORTUNITIES FOR study in the history of technology. The Burndy Library donation brought in numerous publications and manuscripts concerning technological development which supplemented Smithsonian collections in the field. Other strengths in the history of technology are the Libraries' collections of trade catalogs and world's fair publications.

"Ferris wheel, Midway plaisance." Hubert Howe Bancroft. *The book of the fair.* Chicago and San Francisco, 1893. Gift, Larry Zim World's Fair collection.

This limited folio edition of the standard history of the Chicago World's Columbian Exposition was presented to major officials and sponsors of the fair. Numbered copies were printed on extra-wide paper and supplemented with 100 folio prints, among them photogravures and original signed etchings. The many sumptuous illustrations are fine examples of the golden age of chromolithography.

Electrical Engineering and Magnetism

At the core of the Burndy Library donation are materials following the observation of electrical and magnetic phenomena, the design of apparatus for experiments, and practical applications in the fields of navigation, communication, and energy resources. From manuscripts relating to the first experiments of the 1500s to William Gilbert's *De magnete* [On the magnet] (1600) and on to the many publications of Alexander Graham Bell documenting the invention of the wireless telegraph in 1897, these Special Collections holdings are a major resource for the study of the history of science and technology.

"Bureau centrale téléphonique" [Telephone exchange]. Louis Figuier, *Les nouvelles conquetes de la science* [The new conquests of science]. Paris, 1883–85. Gift of the Burndy Library.

The explosion of technological and industrial applications of scientific discoveries in the 1880s is demonstrated by books such as Figuier's multivolume description of the wonders of nineteenth-century life. Figuier, editor of l'Année scientifique *[The scientific year], produced many popular science books.*

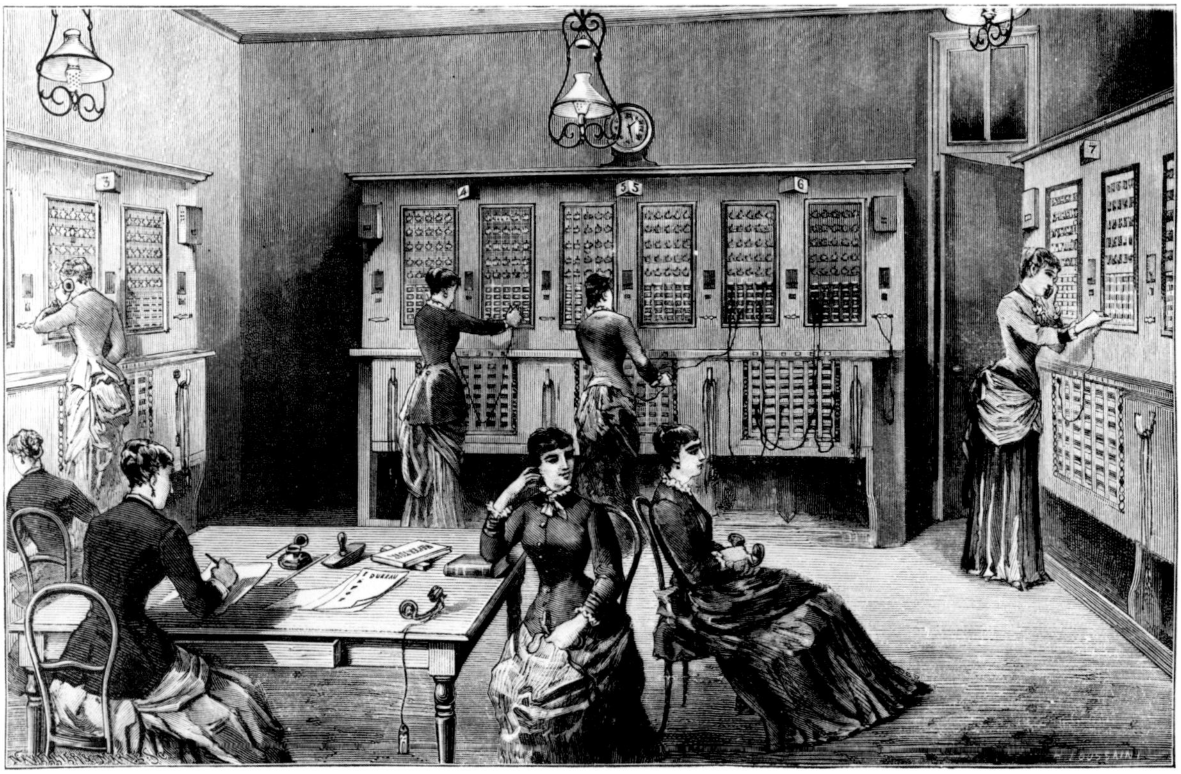

erme le Saucisson
s

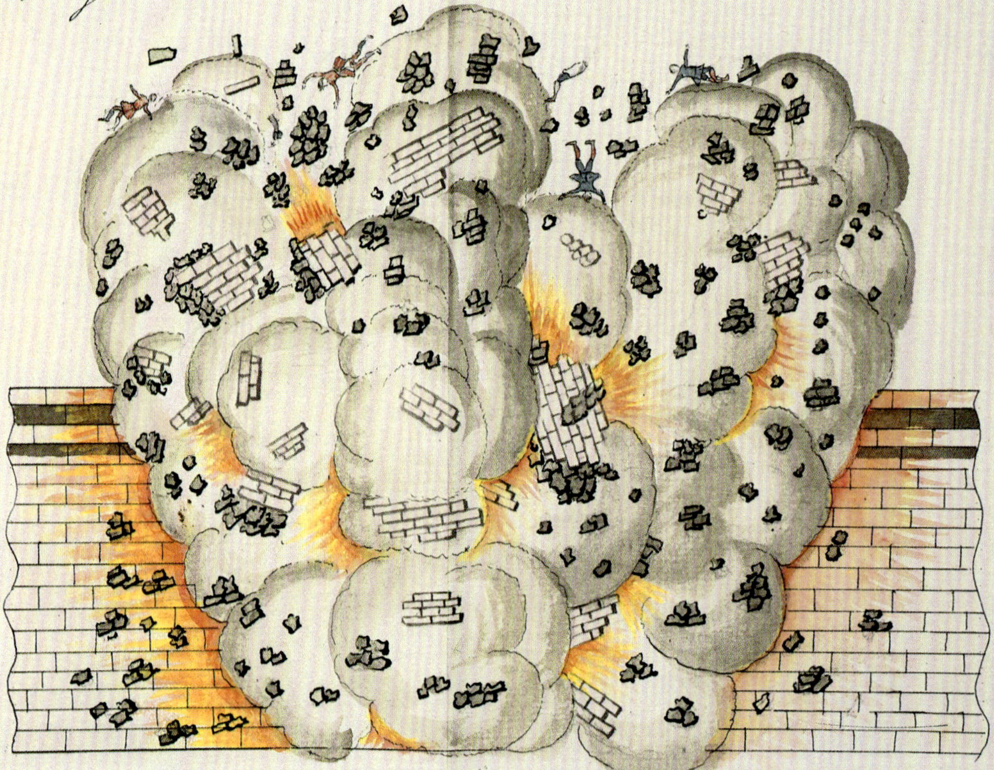

Mechanical and Civil Engineering

The "machine books"—massive illustrated works which describe machines designed primarily to make life easier—are a unique contribution to technological literature. Agostino Ramelli's *Le diverse et artificiose machine* [The diverse and ingenious machinery] (1588) includes many proposed mechanisms which may never have been built. A series of original drawings, apparently made for this publication, are among the Dibner Library's treasures.

Most of the machine books in the Libraries' Special Collections date from the Renaissance and early-modern period, before steam power had been harnessed for use in construction. One prized volume from the Burndy Library donation is Domenico Fontana's 1679 *Della trasportatione dell'obelisco Vaticano* [On the transportation of the Vatican obelisk]. In the engineering bid that won him the contract for the work, Fontana describes how an Egyptian obelisk could be moved from the Circus Maximus to Saint Peter's Square, the Vatican.

The steam power that drove the industrial revolution also influenced transportation and trade. An American contribution to this literature is James Rumsey's *Short Treatise on the Application of Steam* (Philadelphia, 1788). Two unusual multivolume compilations document the history of railroads: J. Elfreth Watkins's proofs for his unpublished *History of the Pennsylvania Railroad Company* (planned for 1896) and the Pullman Company's *Descriptive List of Cars,* partly in print and partly in manuscript form (1900–42).

Books of architecture and civil engineering add breadth to the collection. Construction proposals, commemorative publications, and similar works by military engineers provide a variety of research materials. Engineering and architecture merge in representative texts and manuscripts from the Renaissance rediscovery of the ancient Roman Vitruvius to George Rennie's *Views of the Old and New London Bridges* (1830).

"Des Effets des Mines": "Vue de front d'une mine qui joue" [The effects of mines: Front view of a mine which is exploding] (detail). Sébastien le Prestre de Vauban. "Traité des sièges et de l'attaque des places. . . . Traité de la deffense [sic] des places" [Treatise on sieges and attack of positions. . . . Treatise on the defense of positions]. Manuscript, [ca. 1700]. Gift of the Burndy Library.

Vauban was a late Renaissance engineer whose knowledge of siege warfare assisted a number of rulers. Evidence of patronage indicates that this copy may have been presented to the Duke of Burgundy, whose grandfather Vauban had served, before the work was published.

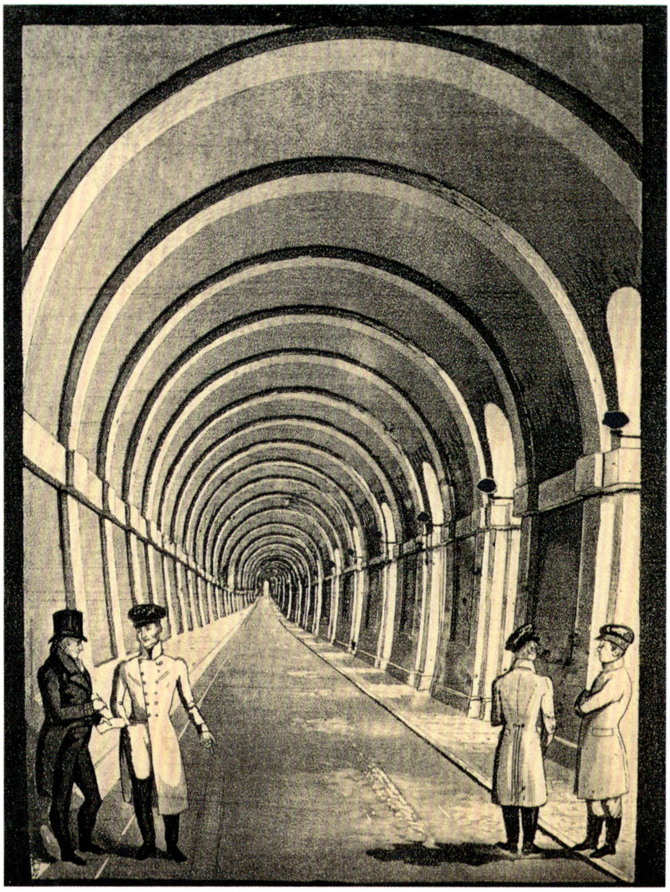

Description des travaux entreprise pour la construction de la tonnelle ou passage sous la Tamise entre Rotherhithe et Wapping [Description of the works undertaken for the construction of the tunnel or passageway under the Thames between Rotherhithe and Wapping]. London, 1840. Gift of the Burndy Library.

This brochure was written for French-speaking visitors to the construction site of the first modern submarine tunnel. The building of the Thames tunnel, which is still in use as part of Britain's rail system, attracted many tourists who came to witness this marvel of invention.

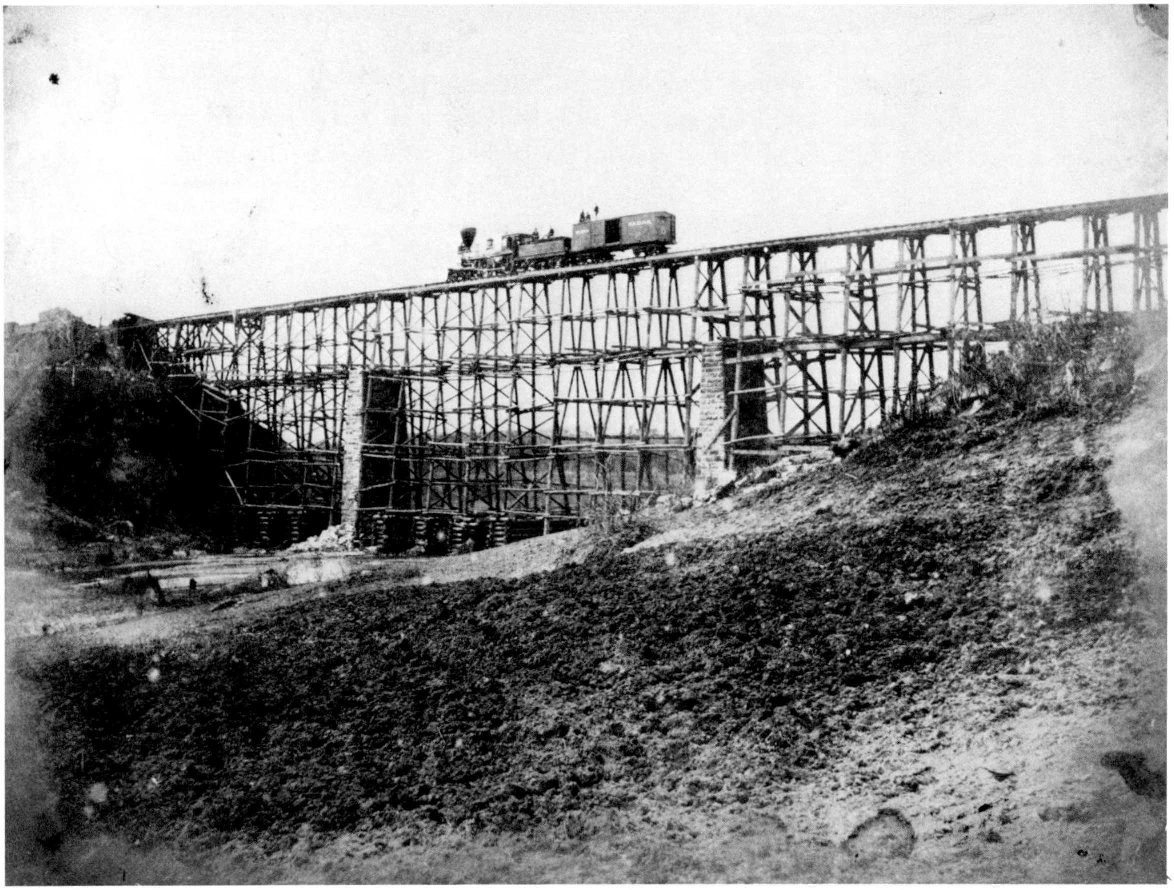

"Military railroad bridge." Herman Haupt. *Photographs illustrative of operations in construction and transportation: as used to facilitate the movements of the armies of the Rappahannock, of Virginia, and of the Potomac.* Boston, 1863.

Haupt's contributions to American engineering covered many fields, with particular distinction in bridge construction. He served in the Civil War as aide-de-camp to General Irwin MacDowell and had responsibility for railroad construction and transportation. The very early photographs in this album document the role of the engineer in American military actions.

Flight

The seventeenth-century biologist Giovanni Alfonso Borelli, in his 1680 work *De motu animalium* [On the movement of animals], tried to quantify the movement of birds and other animals. His studies laid the groundwork for the nineteenth-century contributions of Etienne Jules Marey, who used photography to record and study the flight of birds.

Basic research by scientists such as Robert Boyle and Joseph Priestley, who studied the physics of air and worked out the composition and behavior of gases, led to a new era in human transportation. Their experiments enabled the Montgolfier brothers of France and other adventurous innovators to build balloons which rose and took man into the air.

Man's first flights in heavier-than-air machines, early rocketry, and jet-plane experiments are documented in the Libraries' early works on flight. Many colorful and speculative publications on these topics appeared in the 1930s when rocket scientists were making the leap from creating fireworks and military ordnance to developing power sufficient to lift people from the planet.

Rockets used in eighteenth-century celebrations were described in Amedée Frezier's *Traité des feux d'artifice pour la spectacle* [Treatise on fireworks for display] (1747). German speculative and theoretical works, such as Hermann Oberth's *Die rakete zu den planetraumen* [Rockets to planetary space] (1923) and Otto Willi Gail's *Mit raketendraft ins weltenall: vom feurewagen zum raumschiff* [With rockets into space: from fire engine to spaceship] (1928), reflect the futuristic aims of the early space sciences. These volumes are located in the Admiral DeWitt Clinton Ramsey Room, the Libraries' Special Collections facility located adjacent to the National Air and Space Museum Branch Library. Older works relating to chemistry and the physics of air, the scientific basis of early ballooning, are in the Dibner Library.

"A balloon prospect from above the clouds." Thomas Baldwin. *Airopaidia: containing the narrative of a balloon excursion from Chester, the eighth of September 1785.* Chester [England], 1786. Gift of the Burndy Library.

Signing himself "The Aironaut," the author dedicated this account of his two-hour flight to the citizens of Chester, thanking them for their "kind anxiety manifested during my absence." He described this engraved illustration as "a Specimen of Balloon Geography," showing the country between Chester and Warrington in Lancashire, as seen from the balloon in flight.

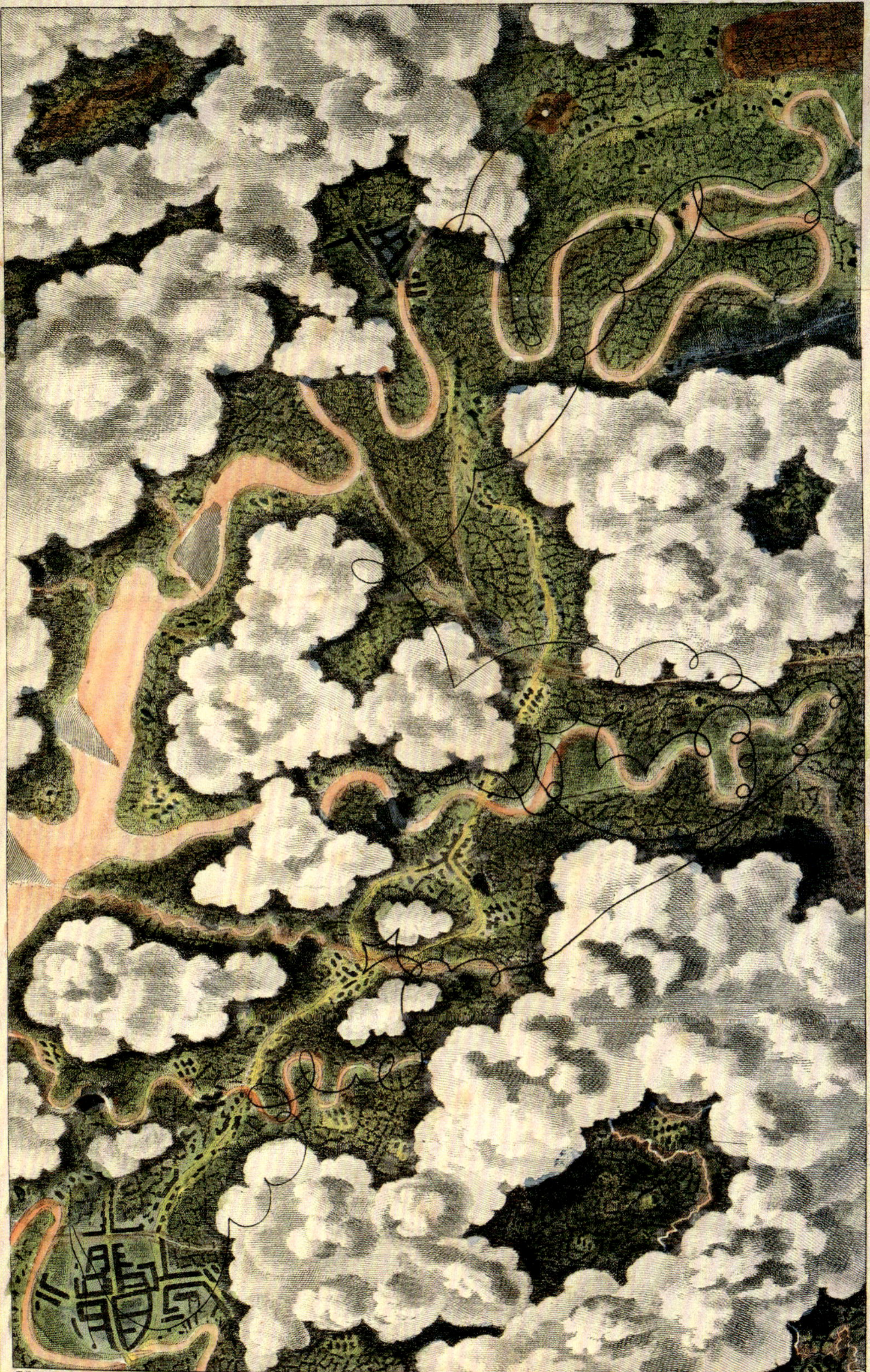

T. Baldwin Arm. del. et pinx. *Angus sculp.*

A **BALLOON PROSPECT** *from* ***ABOVE*** *the* **CLOUDS** *see page* IIII c.

Publish'd May 1st 1786 by T. Baldwin Chester.

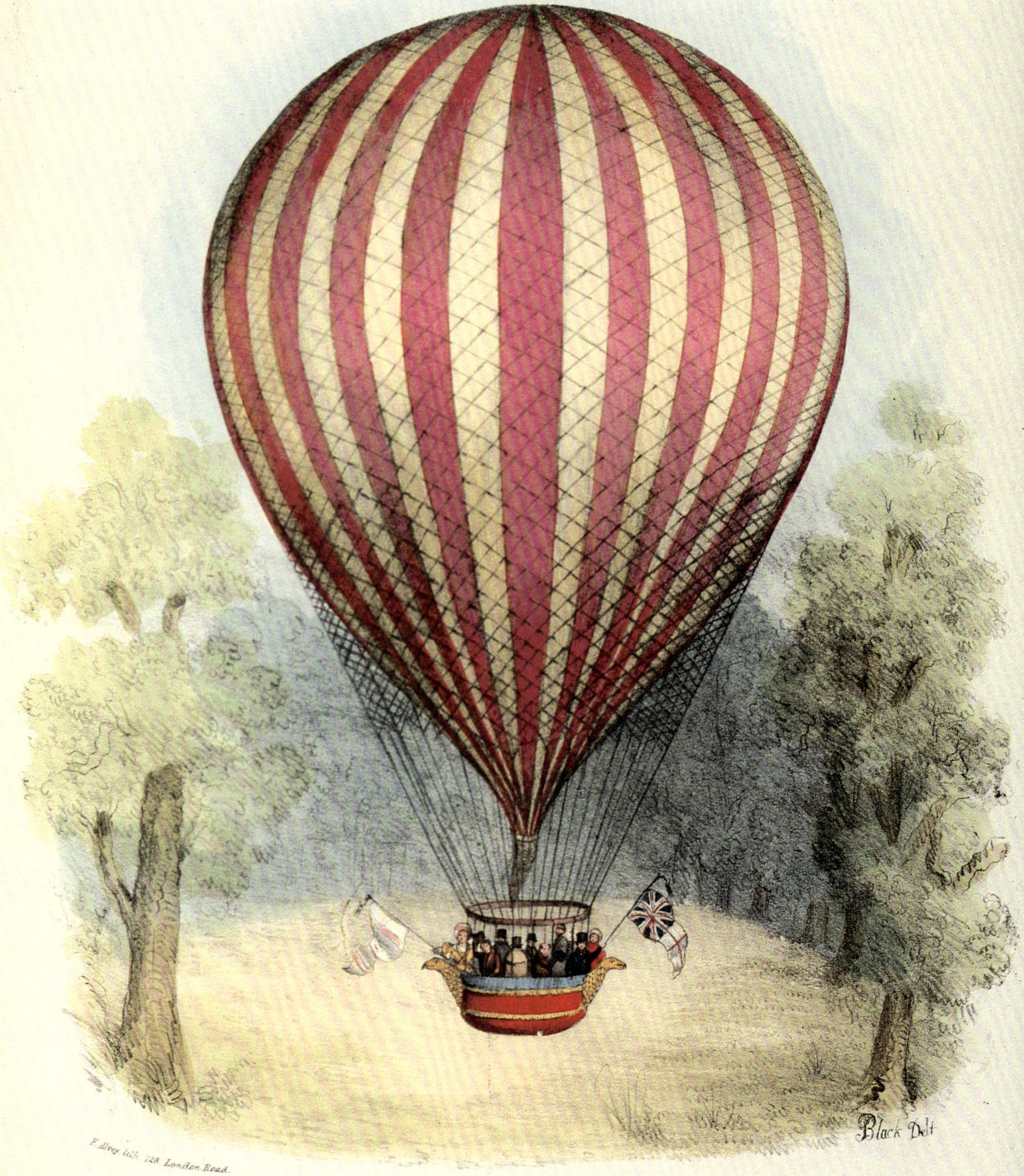

F. Alvey lith. 128 London Road. Black Delt

THE VAUXHALL ROYAL BALLOON.

Formed of 2000 yards of Silk and capable of ascending with Twenty Eight Persons, beside Ballast and Apparatus. Circumference 157 Feet. _ Height, with Car attached, 80 Feet. First Ascent, with 9 Persons, made from Vauxhall September 9th 1836.

London, Published by William Spooner 377. Strand.

"The Vauxhall Royal balloon." William Upcott. [*Scrapbook of early aeronautica.*] [England, 1783–1840]. Gift of Mrs. John Carruthers.

The balloon shown in this lithograph is described as "formed of 2,000 yards of silk and capable of ascending with 28 persons, ballast and apparatus." It first ascended, with nine persons, from London's Vauxhall on September 9, 1836.

Willy Ley. *Die Möglichkeit der Weltraum-Fahrt* [The feasibility of interplanetary travel]. Leipzig, 1928.

Ley, a paleontologist, engineer, and theorist on conditions on other planets and in space, edited this book of essays written by contemporary scientists and engineers, including Hermann Oberth and Guido von Pirquet.

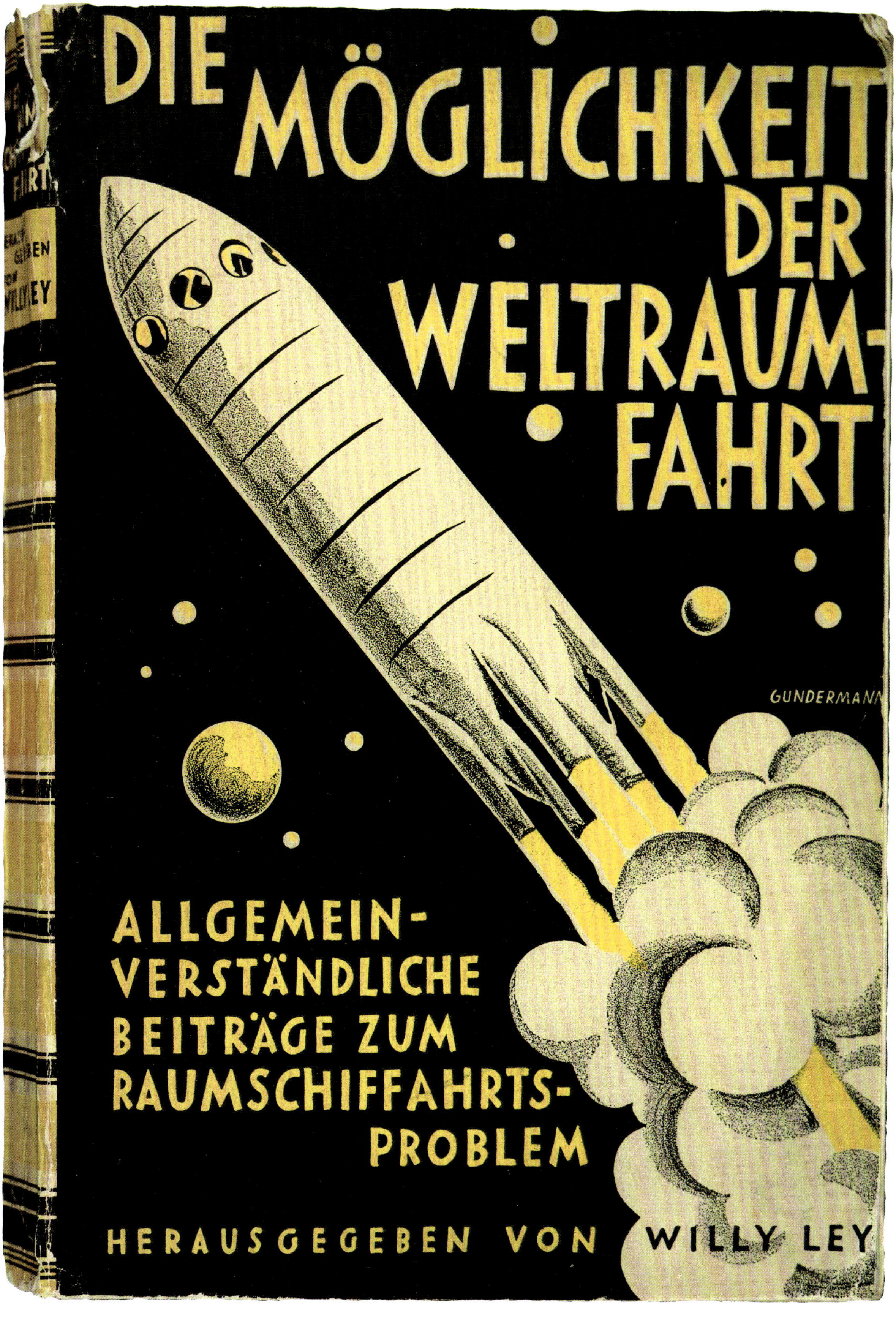
DIE MÖGLICHKEIT DER WELTRAUM-FAHRT
GUNDERMANN
ALLGEMEIN-VERSTÄNDLICHE BEITRÄGE ZUM RAUMSCHIFFAHRTS-PROBLEM
HERAUSGEGEBEN VON WILLY LEY

World's Fairs and International Expositions

One permanent legacy of Smithsonian participation in many of the world's fairs and international expositions held between 1876 and 1914 is a substantial collection of publications. Jury reports, photograph albums, souvenir booklets, exhibitors' catalogs, guidebooks for the public, and special issues of contemporary magazines and periodicals show how great fairs were planned and operated, especially the 1876 Centennial in Philadelphia and the 1893 World's Columbian Exposition in Chicago.

World's fair publications document technological advances, industrial achievements, the changing styles in the fine and decorative arts, popular entertainment, and consumer goods, providing primary material for industrial, economic, social, and cultural historians. In 1989, the Libraries received a gift from the Larry Zim World's Fair Collection of significant publications dating from the 1851 Great Exposition in London's Crystal Palace through the 1986 Vancouver World Exposition, adding depth to the already rich world's fair collection.

"Group of glass, by Count Harrach of Bohemia." Matthew Digby Wyatt. *The industrial arts of the nineteenth century. A series of illustrations of the choicest specimens produced by every nation, at the Great Exhibition of Works of Industry, 1851.* London, 1851–53.

As official secretary to the executive committee of the Great Exhibition, Wyatt drew on the seemingly inexhaustible riches of the exhibits for this major contribution to exhibition literature. An architect, designer, and writer on art, he collaborated in the creation of the exhibits with engineer Isambard Brunel and designer Owen Jones. Both Wyatt and Jones, who influenced generations of artists and designers, adapted the artistic heritage of peoples all over the world for their designs.

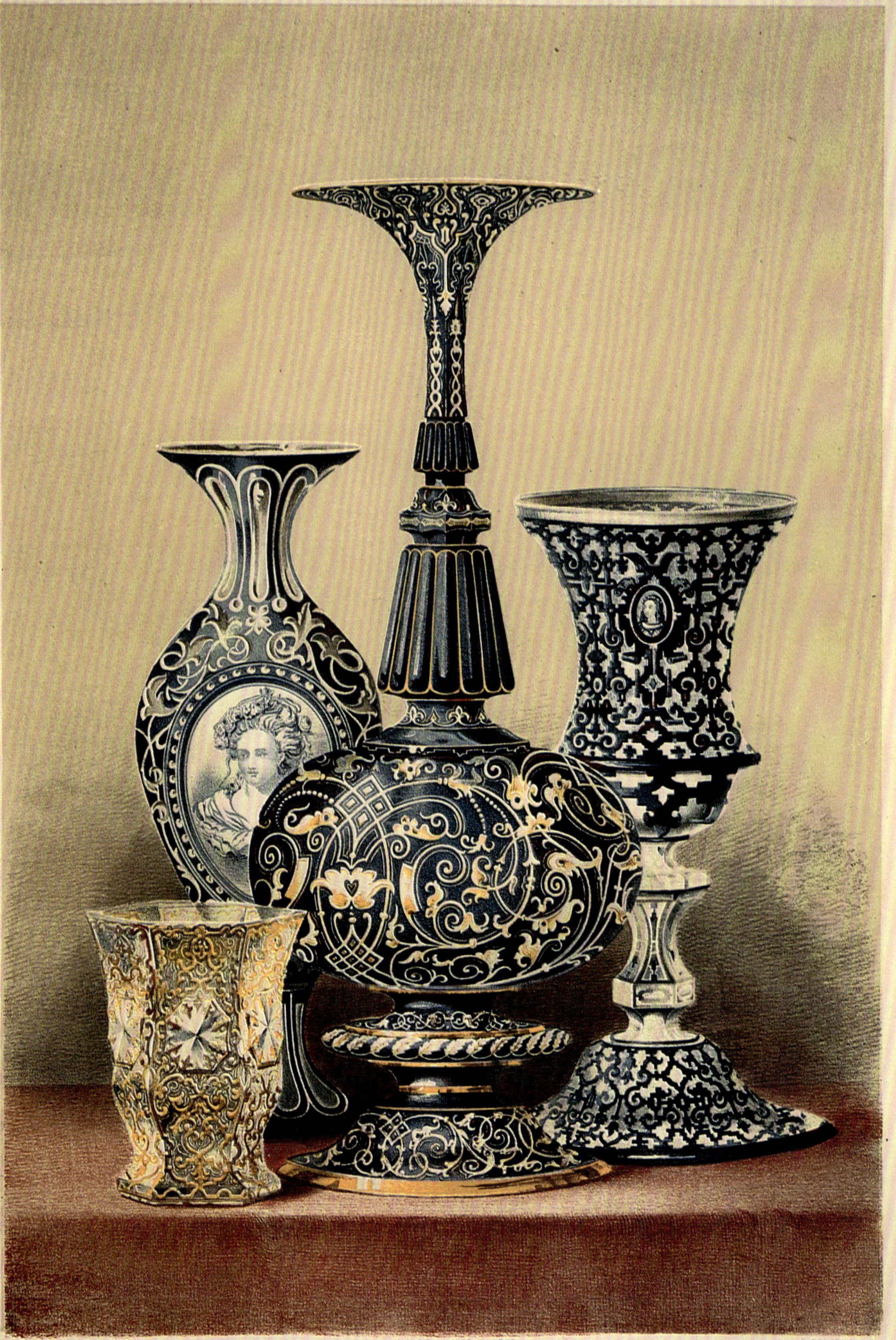

H. N. HUMPHREYS, DEL. M. DIGBY WYATT, DIREXT. F. BEDFORD, LITH.

GROUP OF GLASS, BY COUNT HARRACH OF BOHEMIA

LONDON, PRINTED AND PUBLISHED FEBY 15TH 1852 BY DAY & SON LITHOGRAPHERS TO THE QUEEN

TRANSVERSE SECTION

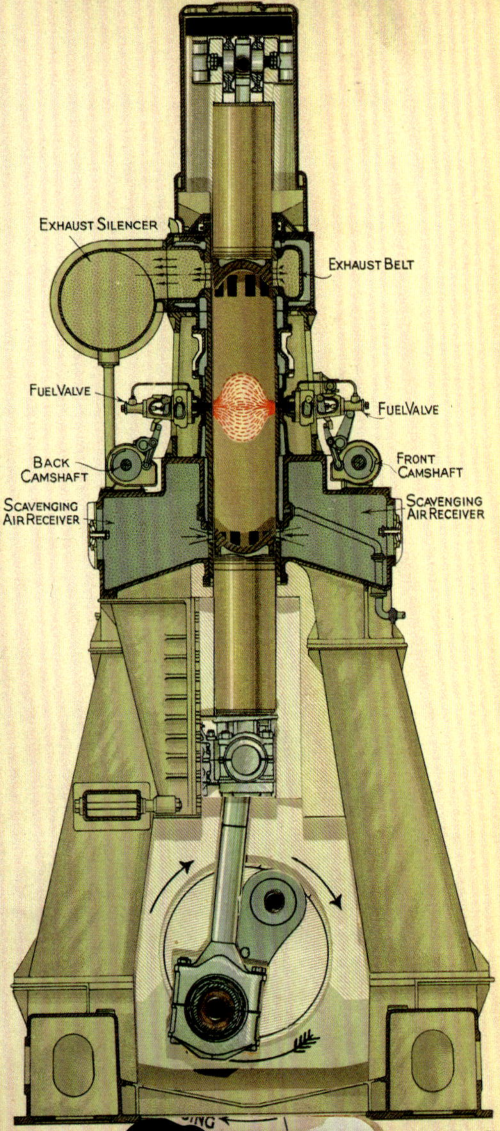

To Work Model Turn Disc Here

White & Pike Ltd. Model Specialists, Birmingham.

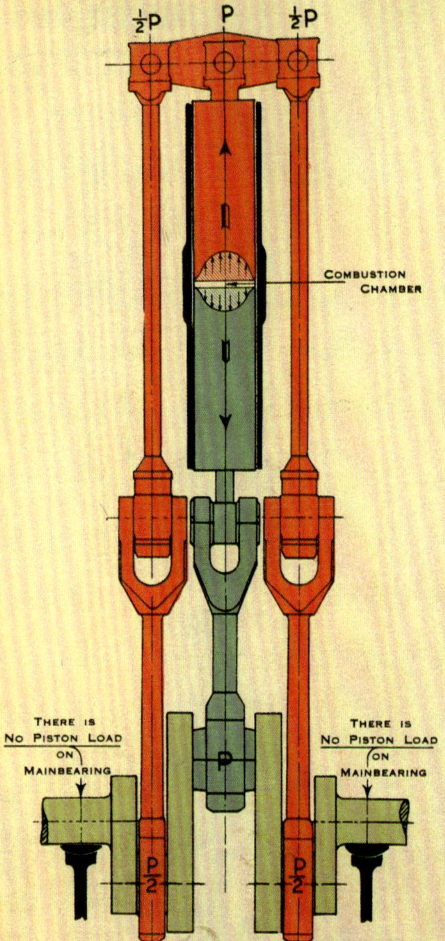

DIAGRAM SHEWING LOAD ON THE TWO PISTONS PASSING DIRECT THROUGH THREE CONNECTING RODS TO THREE CRANKS. - - - MAINBEARINGS LOCATING AND SUPPORTING CRANKSHAFT AND RUNNING GEAR.

P.T.O.

Trade Literature

The Special Collections include a national treasure of over 285,600 pieces of trade literature, representing 35,000 companies, which document the history of business, labor, industry, and technology. Both a product of and an index to industrialization and mass production, the collection includes technical manuals, company histories, instructions for using products, testimonials from satisfied customers, advertising catalogs, pattern and design books, price lists, and internal factory record books.

In the Libraries' collections the early development of machines can be traced from the scarce sale lists published by the eighteenth-century English instrument-maker George Adams and other skilled artisans who built the early machines. These lists were predecessors to the manufacturing company catalogs of the late nineteenth century.

Manufacturers' catalogs in the collections include descriptions of such diverse subjects as the sewing machine, the layout of a German pencil factory, and flapper fashions of the 1920s. The catalogs also document the manufacturing history of specific machines, successive adjustments and innovations, and the phasing out of early models, techniques, and materials.

Donations from several university libraries and from the Center for Research Libraries, a gift of 60,000 catalogs on machine-tooling and metalworking collected by businessman Mel Heinz, and purchase of catalogs formerly owned by the Franklin Institute have created probably the largest existing collection of trade catalogs and related material accessible to scholars.

Opposite: Doxford & Sons, Ltd. *Doxford opposed piston oil engine.* Sunderland [England], [1922?].

This ingenious trade advertisement has six layers of paper and board which were used to produce movable parts.

Page 66: R. H. Shumway. *R. H. Shumway's 1900 illustrated garden guide.* Rockford, Ill., 1900.

Page 67: Sears, Roebuck & Co. *Honor-bilt modern homes.* [Chicago], 1930.

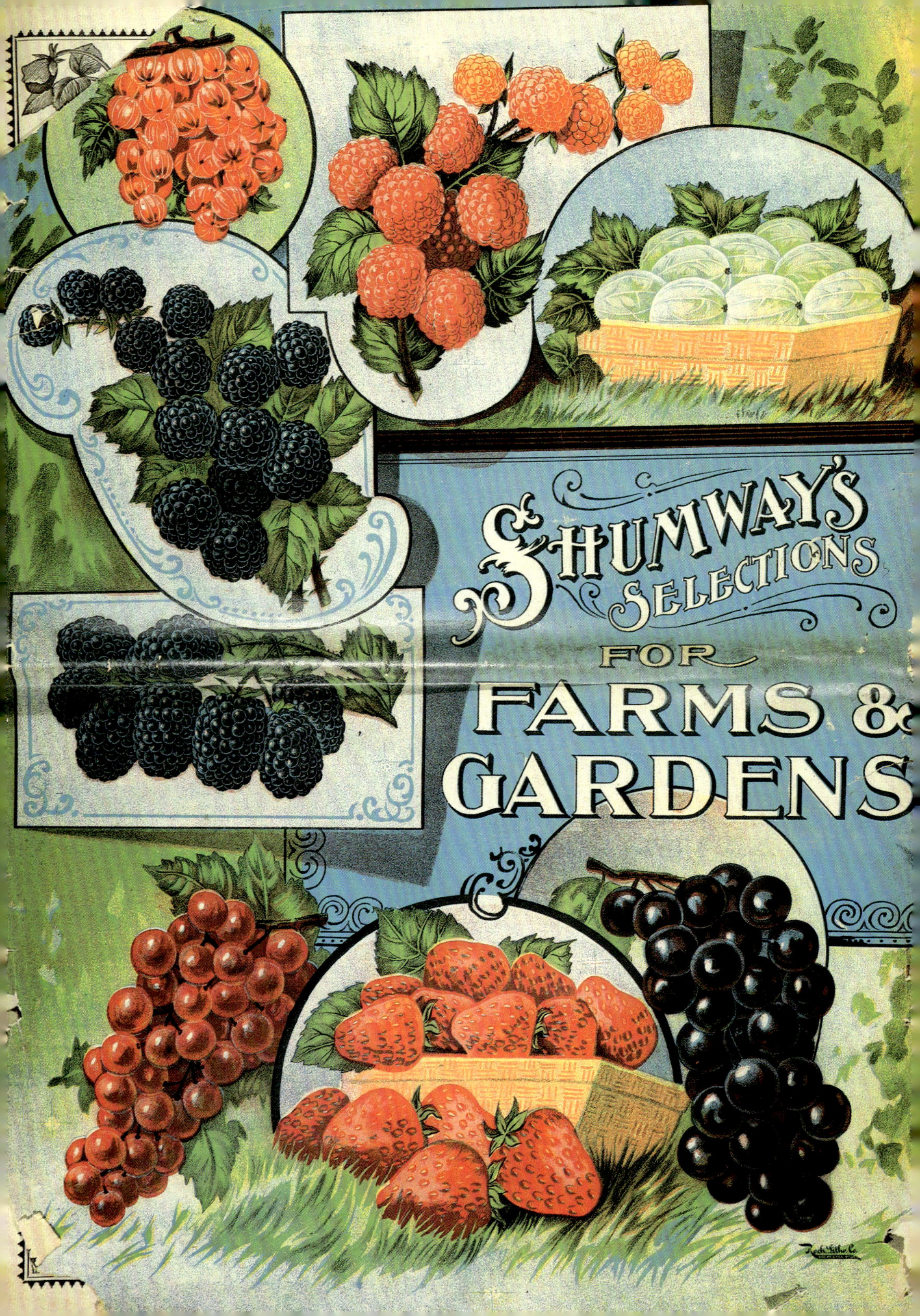
SHUMWAY'S
SELECTIONS
FOR
FARMS &
GARDENS

Honor Bilt MODERN HOMES

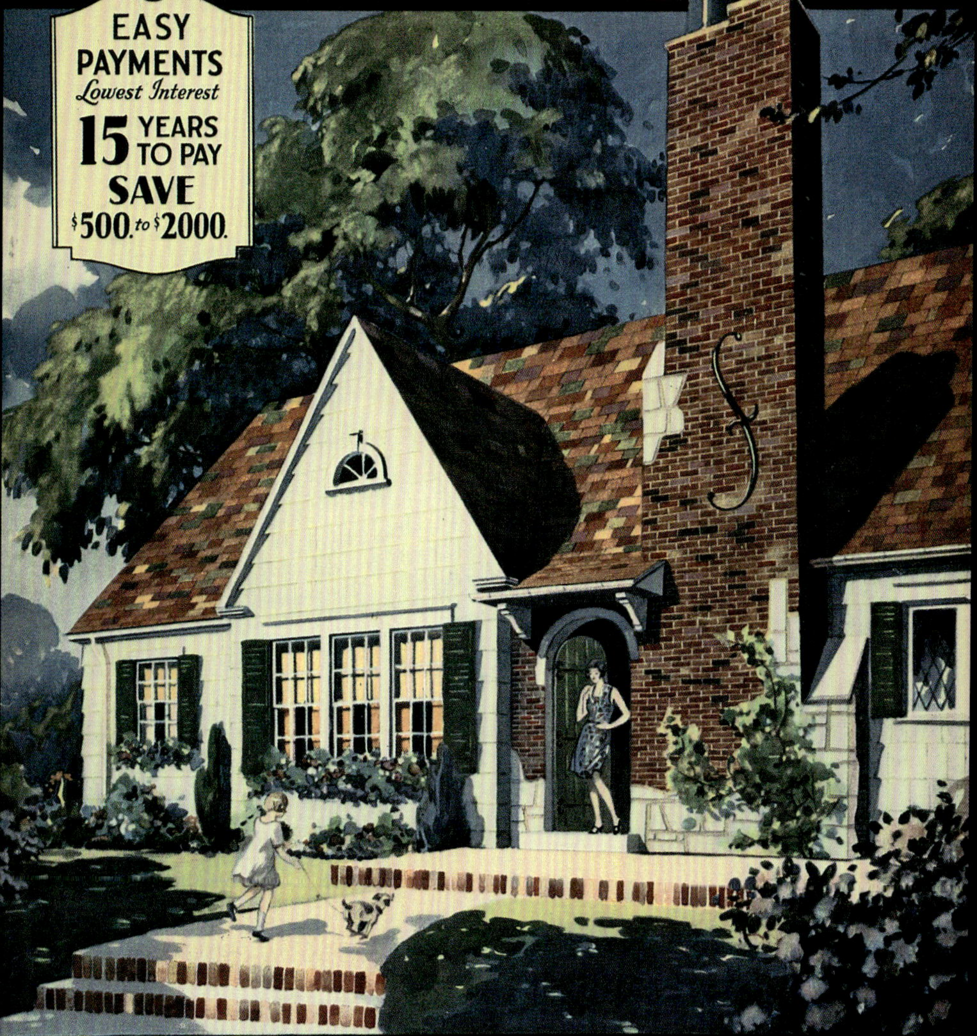

Sears, Roebuck *and* Co.

The World's Largest Builders of Fine Homes

Natural History

AT THE TIME THE SMITHSONIAN WAS FOUNDED, THE PRIMARY interest of natural scientists was the classic collections-based research of taxonomy and systematics. Taxonomy is the science of identifying and naming species and higher groups; systematics is that of classifying or organizing species into such groups by their evolutionary relationships. Both require extensive observation and documentation in the field and meticulous study in museum collections. Taxonomy and systematics continue to be the basis for other scientific research—on, for example, endangered species, biodiversity, and tropical ecosystems. Now aided by powerful modern technologies, scientists at the National Museum of Natural History, the National Zoological Park, the Smithsonian Environmental Research Center, the Museum Support Center, and the Smithsonian Tropical Research Institute in Panama continue to rely on the physical examination of specimens and consultation of the historical literature when carrying out much of their research.

"Alcyonium arboreum." Eugen Johann Christoph Esper. *Die Pflanzethiere in Abbildungennach der Natur* [Zoophytes in illustrations from nature]. Nuremberg, 1791–[1830].

Hand-colored engravings like this dominated natural history illustration from the 1600s into the 1800s. They required the special skills of the engraver or etcher as well as the separate, labor-intensive work of coloring each copy of the print by hand. The technique was supplanted by lithography in the nineteenth century.

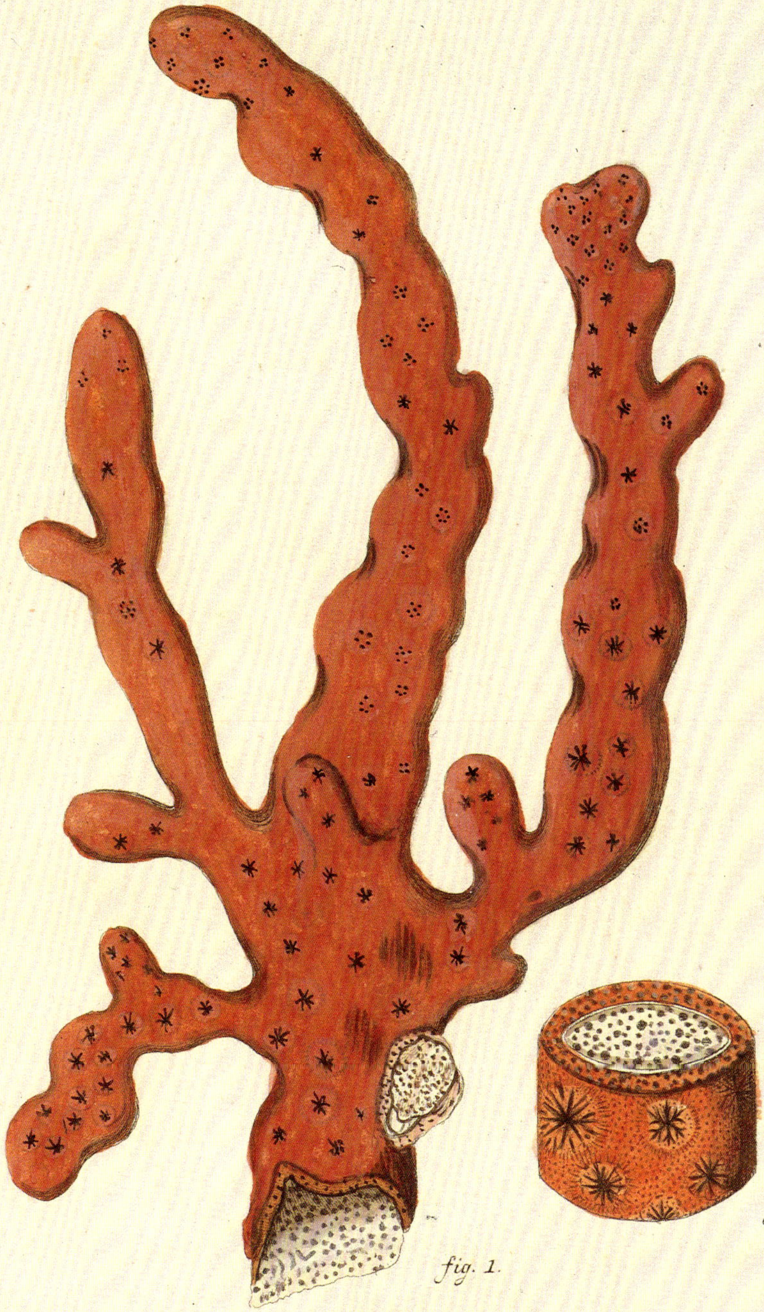

fig. 1.

fig. 2.

Alcyonium arboreum.
Linn. *sp.* 1. Pall. *sp.* 3.

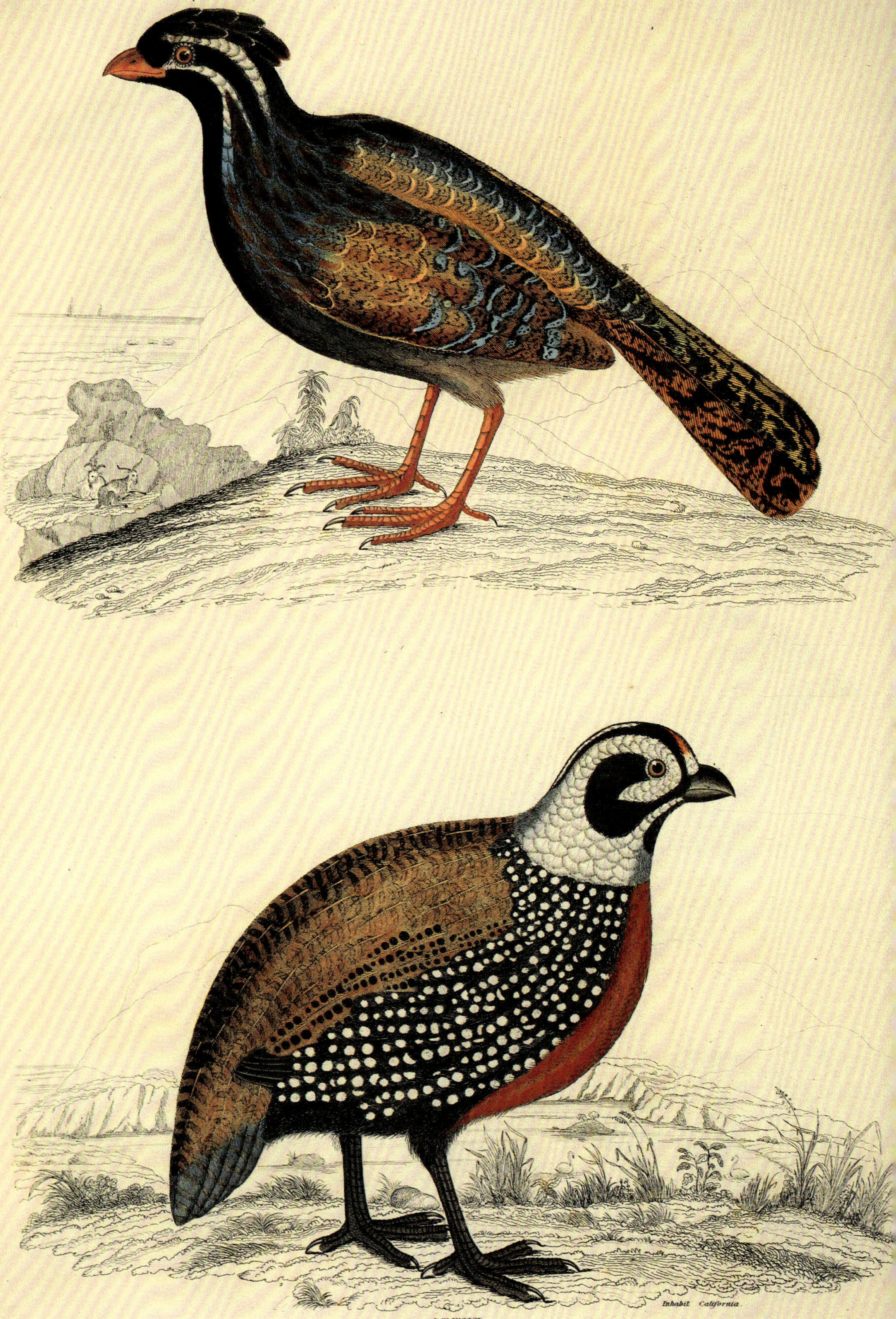

Drawn by Captain Brown.

ORTYX.
QUAILS.

1. Long-Tailed Quail .... O. Macroura.
2. Montezuma's D°. .... Montezumæ.

Zoology

The Libraries' collections supporting zoological research—the collection, study, classification, and care of vertebrate and invertebrate animals—start with early printed works of the classical writers and the encyclopedic publications of Konrad Gesner, Ulisse Aldrovandi, and Albert Seba from the early years of modern science.

Among the Libraries' treasures are the works of Carl von Linné, known also as Linnaeus, the eighteenth-century Swedish botanist and zoologist who developed a system of classification and nomenclature for animals that was adopted throughout Europe. Special Collections holds many editions and translations of his masterwork *Systema naturæ* [The system of nature], including the notable tenth edition (Stockholm, 1758), which remains the foundation of systematics.

The explosion of zoological knowledge in the 1800s found visual expression in scientific publications that are also beautiful picture books. Spectacular hand-colored plates of fishes, insects, corals, and innumerable other animals illuminate large folio volumes which are still consulted by Smithsonian researchers for both their illustrations and their scientific descriptions. Special Collections holdings are especially strong in illustrated works on birds, shells, and butterflies, among them the magnificent ornithological works of John Gould and Daniel Giraud Elliot.

The Libraries generally and its Special Collections specifically have benefited from the generosity of the Institution's scientists. Among the many distinguished private library collections donated over the years are those of zoologist Spencer F. Baird; malacologist William H. Dall; ornithologists Charles W. Richmond and Alexander Wetmore; and mammalogist and paleontologist Remington Kellogg. Such donations and bequests from curators and other staff continue. Outstanding gifts which have added great depth to the zoological resources include rare ornithological works from John H. Phipps and Marcia Brady Tucker.

"Ortyx. Quails." Thomas Brown. *Illustrations of the game birds of North America.* Edinburgh, [1835]. Gift of John H. Phipps.

This plate combines hand-colored engraving of the bird figures with black-and-white etching of the background. It is one of five plates in this extremely rare work that depict species new to science.

J.J.N.A. Spalowski. *Prodromus in systema historicum testaceorum* [Introduction to the systematic classification of shells]. Vienna, 1795.

A jewel in the research collections, this volume has many life-size illustrations in hand-colored plates of 122 species. Among the rarest of published books on mollusks, this is a valuable research tool because it contains descriptions of new species. Mollusks pictured on this plate are found in the waters of western Mexico, Panama, Peru, the Caribbean, and Florida as well as in parts of the south Pacific and western Atlantic. The purchase of this very rare book was made possible by a grant from the Smithsonian Institution Collections Acquisition Fund with additional funds from the Libraries' Special Collections Endowment and the Museum of Natural History's Division of Mollusks.

T.V.

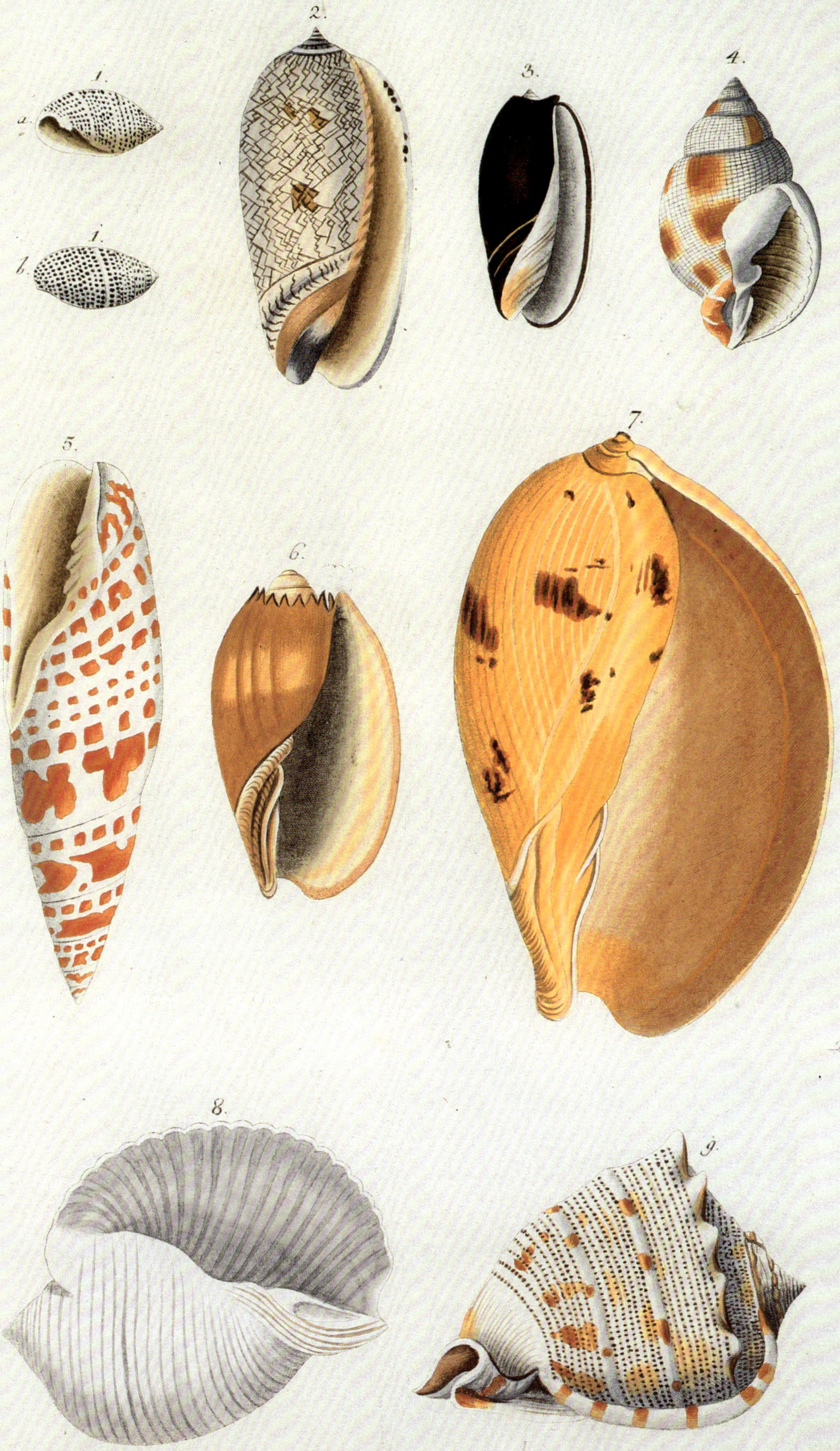

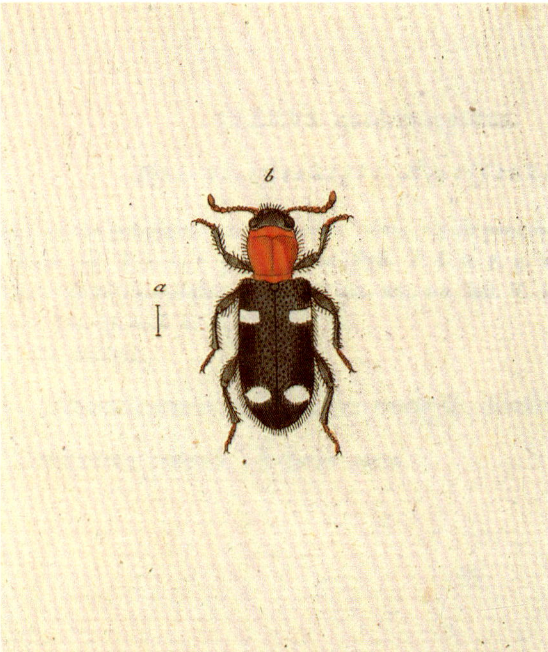

Clerus quadrimaculatus Fabr.

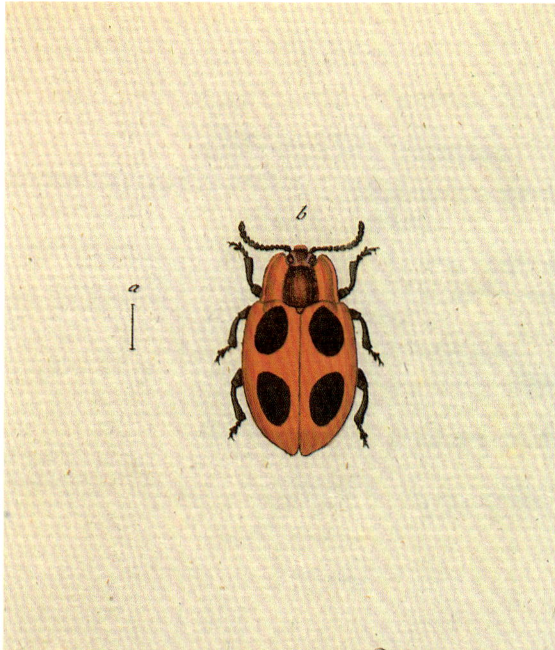

Endomychus coccineus Fabr.

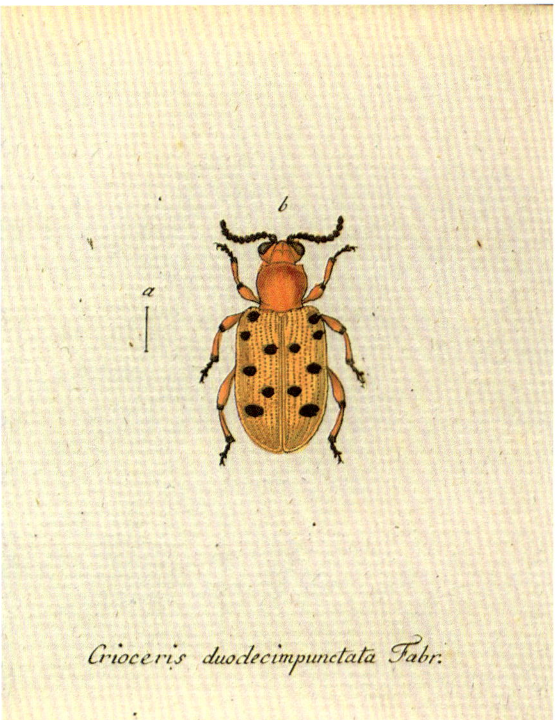

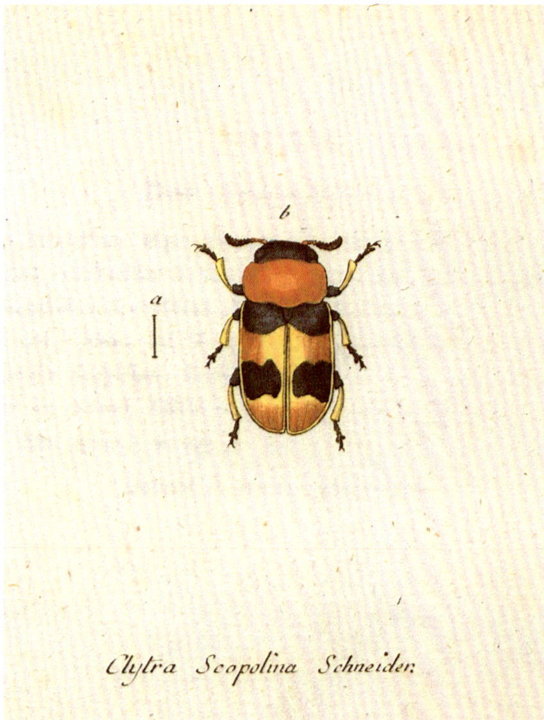

"*Clerus quadrimaculatus* Fabr.; *Endomychus coccineus* Fabr.; *Crioceris duodecimpunctata* Fabr.; *Clytra scopolina* Schneider." Georg Wolfgang Franz Panzer. *Faunæ insectorum germanicæ initia* [The elements of the German insect fauna]. Nuremberg, 1796–1813.

A selection of illustrations from Panzer, each of which was published as an individual plate. Issued in 109 installments over eighteen years, this work contains some 2,500 hand-colored engraved plates, with brief text for each species illustrated. Each plate presents a single insect life-sized; they were drawn and etched by Jakob Sturm, the finest European entomological artist of his generation.

Botany

The Libraries holds over 400 rare books on botany, many of them renowned for their beauty in a field long known for the quality of its illustration. Within forty years of the invention of printing (ca. 1450), herbals with woodcut illustrations were among the most popular printed books. The Burndy Library donation and that of the American Pharmaceutical Association and Bristol-Myers Squibb augmented the Libraries' botany holdings with a selection of early printed herbals, apothecaries' manuals, and related works.

The usefulness of botanical books depends to a great extent on the accuracy of their plant descriptions and illustrations. In the 1500s Pietro Andrea Mattioli's *Commentarii in sex libros Pedacii Dioscoridis Anazarbei De materia medica* [Commentaries in six books on "De materia medica" [Concerning medicinal substances] of Dioscorides Pedanius of Anazarbos] (Venice, 1544) and Leonhart Fuchs's *De historia stirpium* [On the history of plants] (Basel, 1542) attempted to organize and classify all that was known about plants. These encyclopedic works were among the first to include illustrations based on first-hand observation. Their descriptions and woodcut illustrations were a major advance in the accurate representation of natural objects compared to the static, stereotyped images handed down through centuries of manuscript copying.

Through the 1700s and 1800s, as works by Mark Catesby, Georg Dionysius Ehret, Pierre Joseph Redouté, and many others in Special Collections amply demonstrate, the skills of artist, engraver, etcher, and hand-colorist produced magnificent illustrations of plants and animals as they were being discovered, named, and described by Western science.

"Acorus" [Sweet flag (iris)]. *Herbarius. Incipit tractatus de virtutibus herbarum* [Herbal. Here begins a treatise on the virtues of plants]. Venice, 1499.

Like the medieval manuscript illustrations on which they were modeled, many early printed plant images were static designs simplified to the point of being unrecognizable. This illustration in a traditional herbal is unusually charming and identifiable. Gift of the Burndy Library.

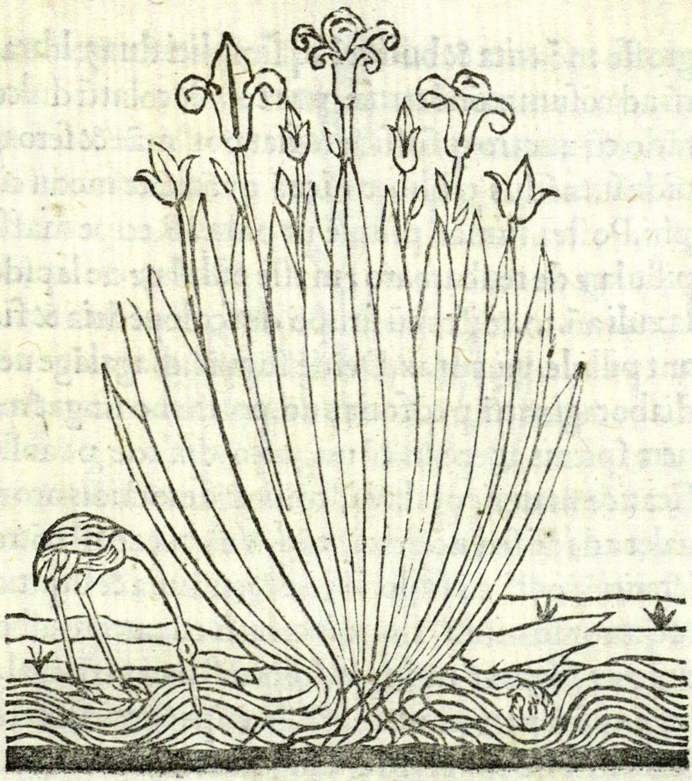

ACORVS

❧ Acorus calidus & sicc᷒ ĩ secũdo. Habet uirtutẽ diureticã dissolutiuã. abstersiuã & apitiuã. Acor᷒ ergo ualet ad dissoluãdũ duriciẽ splenis. & ualet cõtra opilationem splenis & epatis ex causa frigida prouenienté isto modo dispensando. R. radicẽ acori cõquassati quartã lib. humectetur radix ĩ aceto ad tres dies cui adde radicam reupõtici. ʒ. ii. florum boraginis scolopẽdrie añ. m. ʒ. seminis anisi liquiricie añ. ʒ. ii. uuarum passularum. õʒ. ʒ. oĩa

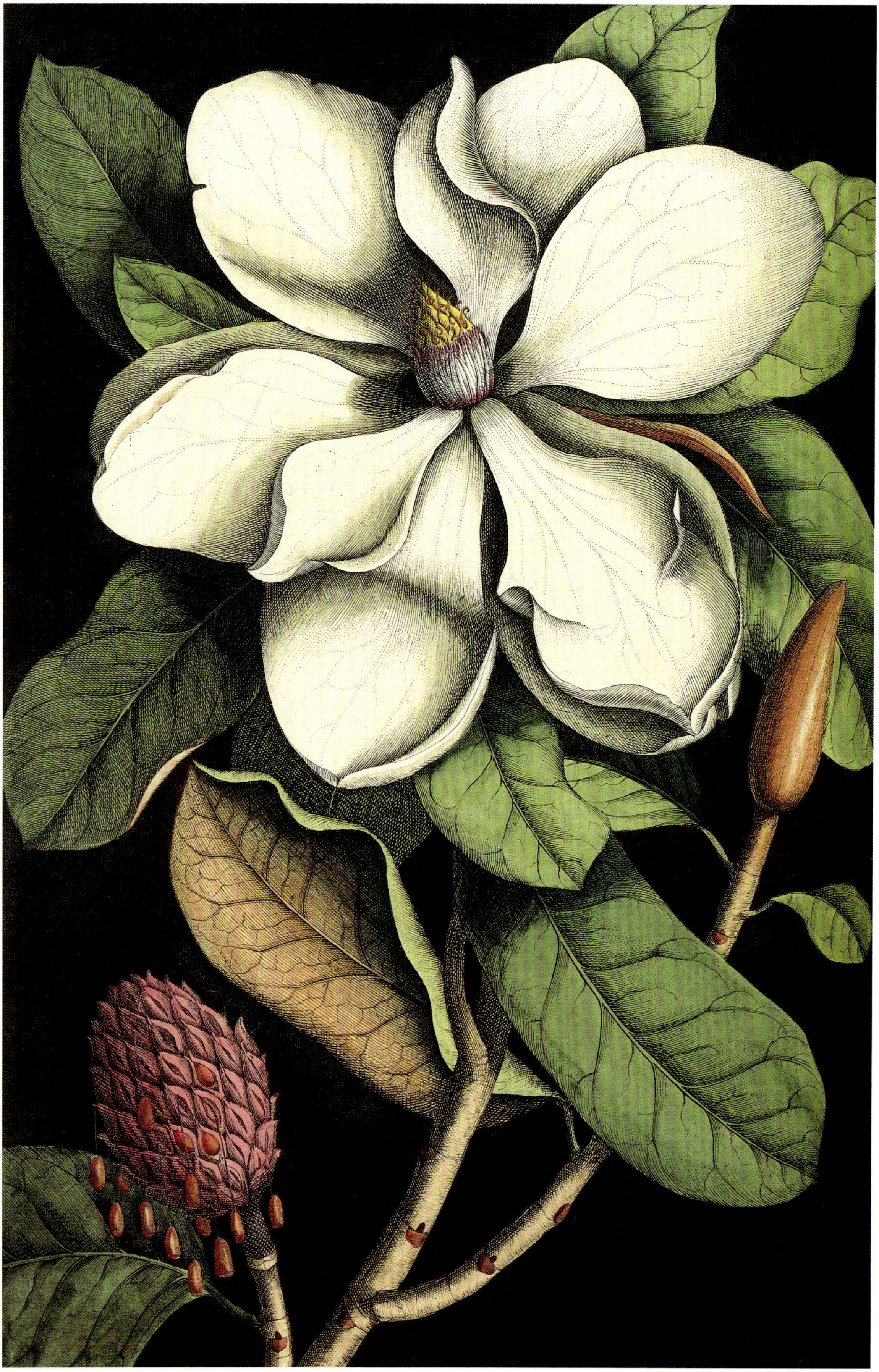

"Magnolia altissima. . . . The Laurel Tree of Carolina." Mark Catesby. *The natural history of Carolina, Florida and the Bahama Islands.* London, 1731–43.

Catesby spent over ten years in the territory which is now the southeastern United States, collecting and sketching specimens, then learned engraving and etching in order to produce his own plates for this two-volume work. He personally hand-colored many of the finished etchings. His was the first color-illustrated account of the flora and fauna of the United States. Its folio size allowed many plants and animals to be depicted life-size. Linnaeus cited this book for approximately seventy species' names in his Systema naturæ *[System of nature] (10th ed., 1758).*

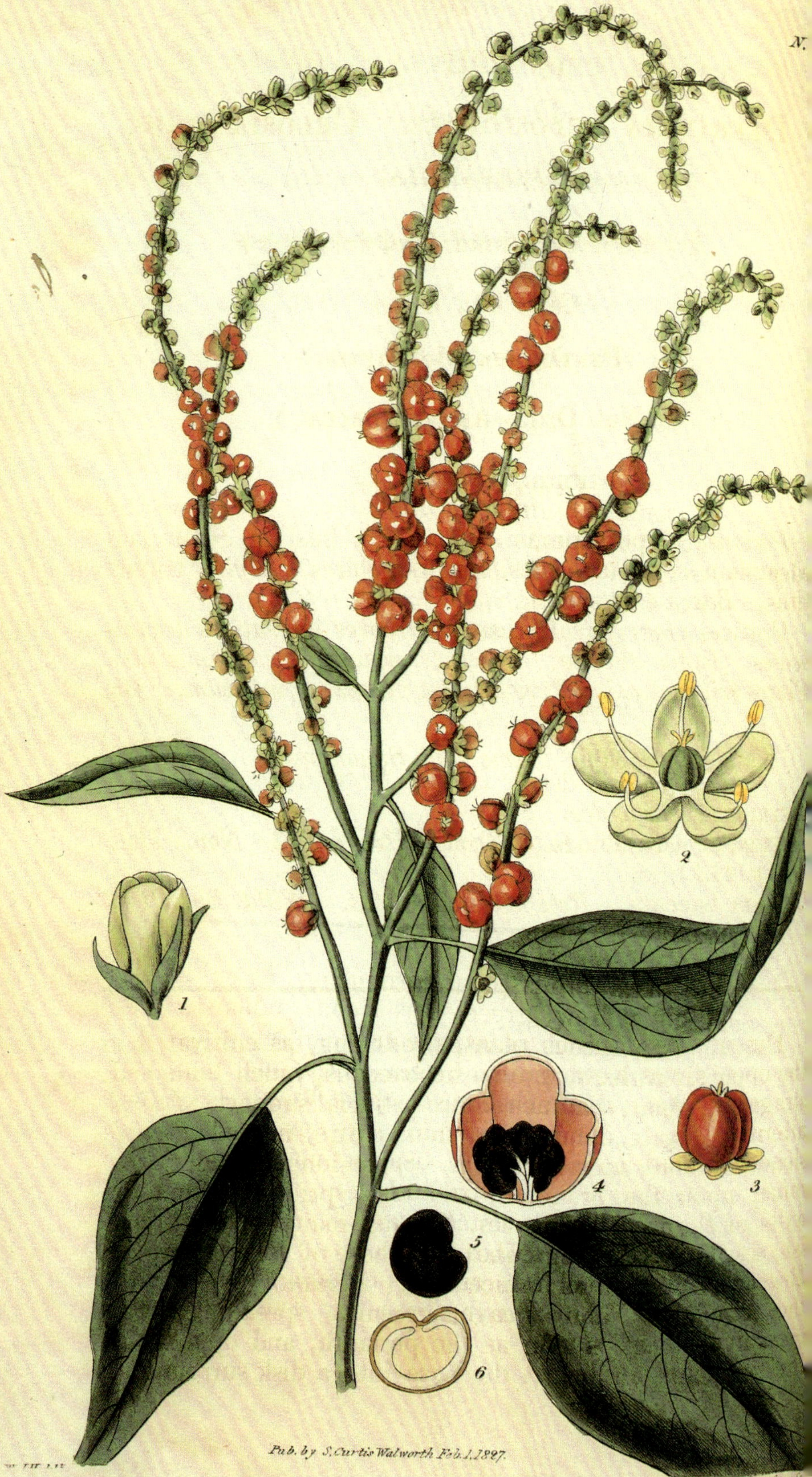

Pub. by S. Curtis Walworth Feb. 1. 1827.

"Deeringia celosioides. Celosia-like Deeringia." William Curtis, ed. *Curtis's botanical magazine, or, Flower-garden displayed.* London, 1827.

Curtis was affiliated with Kew Gardens, the primary botanical garden in England with major experimental and acclimatization interests. The magazine, established in 1787 to describe and illustrate the many new exotic species being brought back to England by exploring expeditions, is the oldest scientific journal in continuous publication.

Voyages and Expeditions

The years 1700–1900 were a period of great scientific voyages. Many governments sponsored expeditions that carried geographers, naturalists, and artists all over the world. These voyages brought back to their patrons and museums at home countless specimens of plants and animals and cultural objects from previously little-known lands. Naturalists in scientific academies, universities, museums, and botanical gardens then organized the collections and published descriptions and illustrations of the specimens, with special emphasis on those species that were new to Western science. The official accounts and scientific publications resulting from expeditions and voyages are a major strength of the Libraries' Special Collections.

The great United States Exploring Expedition of 1838–42 and later governmental expeditions are the source of many anthropological and natural history collections and the many publications describing them that came to the Smithsonian in its early years. The Smithsonian's Spencer F. Baird, who served as the Director of the U.S. National Museum, Assistant Secretary, and Secretary in the years 1848–86, ensured that U.S. government-sponsored expeditions included properly equipped naturalists and artists. Expeditions were sent out to map the boundaries with Mexico and Canada, to find routes for railroads, and to explore the geological history and resources of the West. The Libraries' collection of these publications includes some volumes inscribed by Smithsonian curators with museum accession numbers that connect the published descriptions of newly discovered species with the actual specimens which are still part of the National Museum of Natural History's collections.

"Pine forest, Oregon." Charles Wilkes. *Narrative of the United States Exploring Expedition.* Philadelphia, 1845.

The United States Exploring Expedition, led by Captain Charles Wilkes, was this country's first major venture in mounting an official voyage. For five years Wilkes explored the west coast of North America and the Pacific Ocean from its arctic to its antarctic waters. He published a five-volume (with atlas) narrative of the expedition, from which this illustration is taken. Over the next thirty years he supervised the publication of fifteen more volumes (plus nine atlases) of scientific studies on the specimens and data that were collected, many of which were eventually deposited at the Smithsonian.

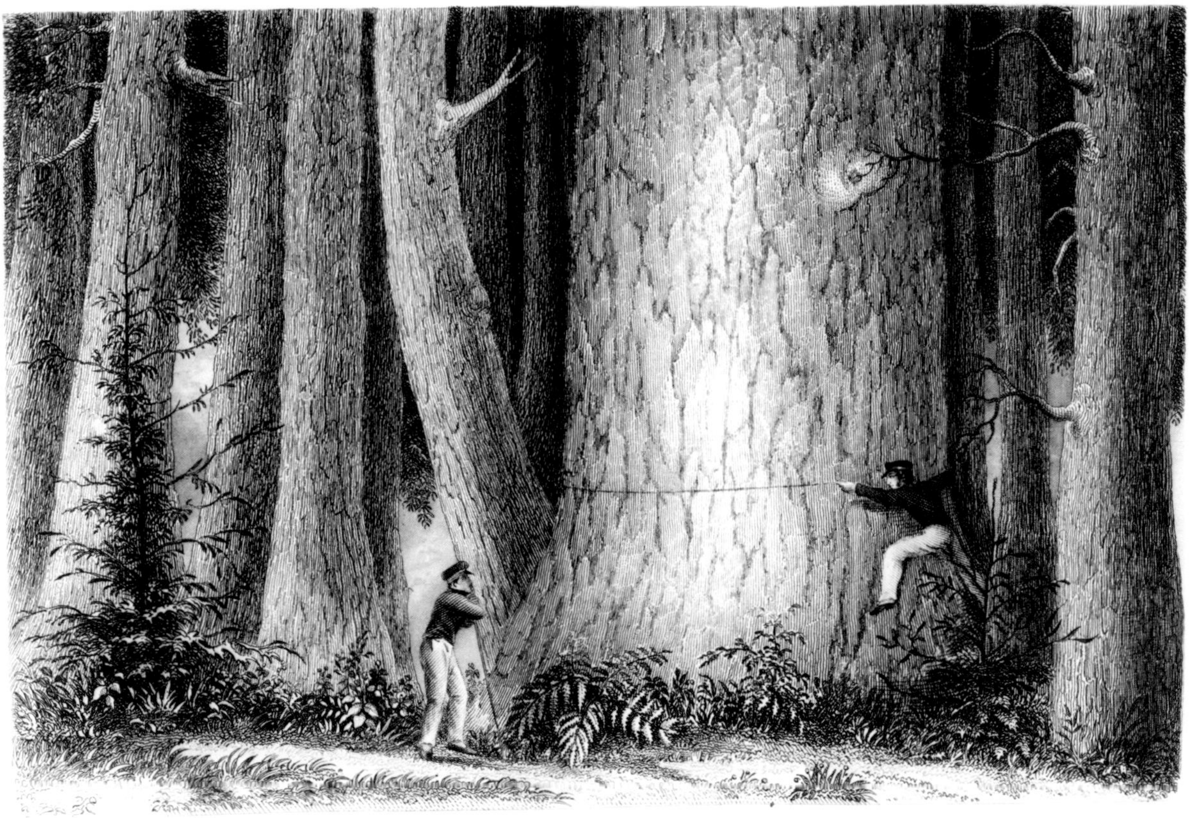

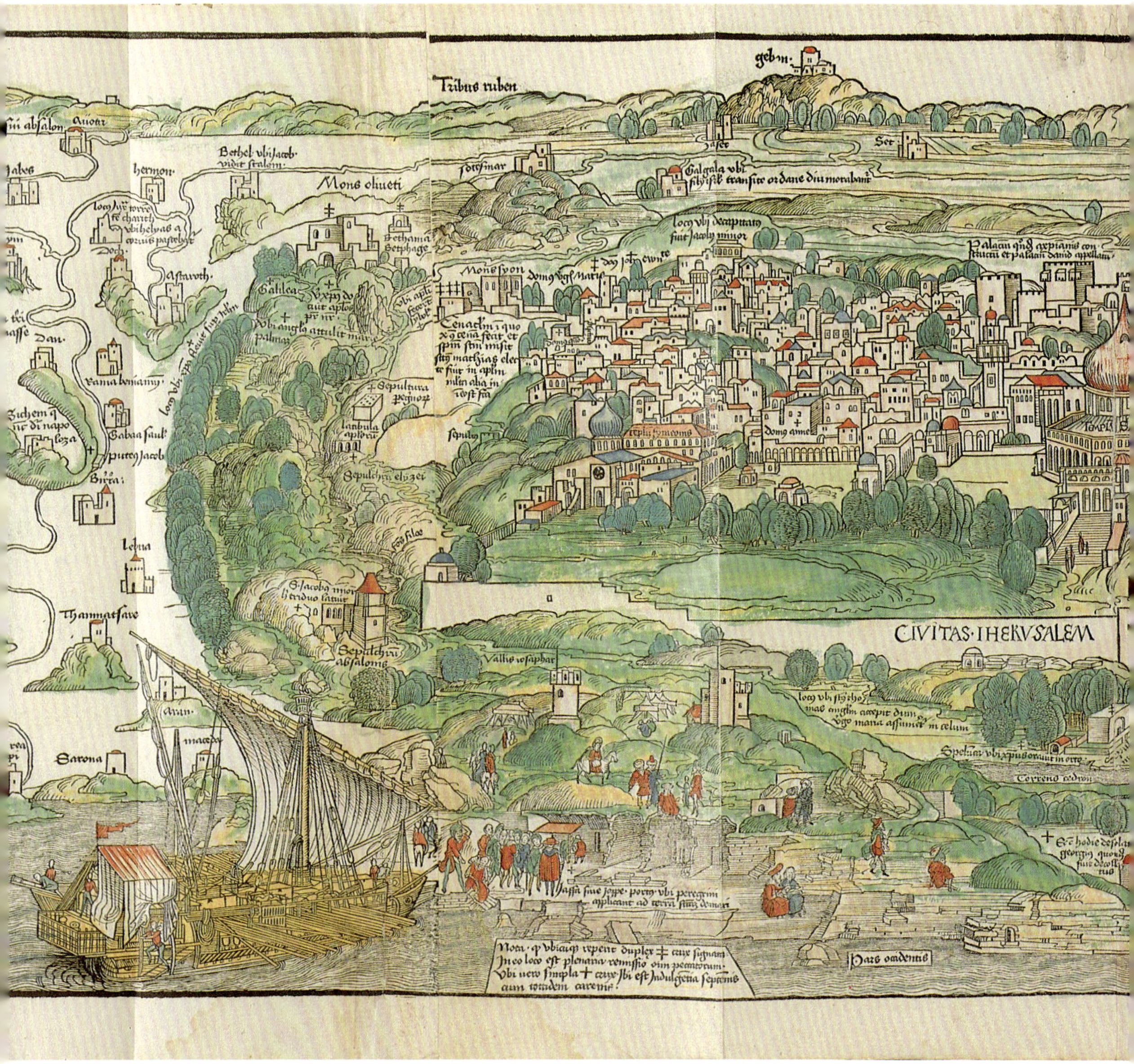
Tribus ruben
Mons olueti
Bethel vbi iacob vidit scalam
hermon
Astaroth
Dan
Sarona
Galgala vbi filii isrl transito iordane diu morabant
Mons syon
Sepulchru absalonis
Vallis iosaphat
CIVITAS · IHERVSALEM
Pars occidentis

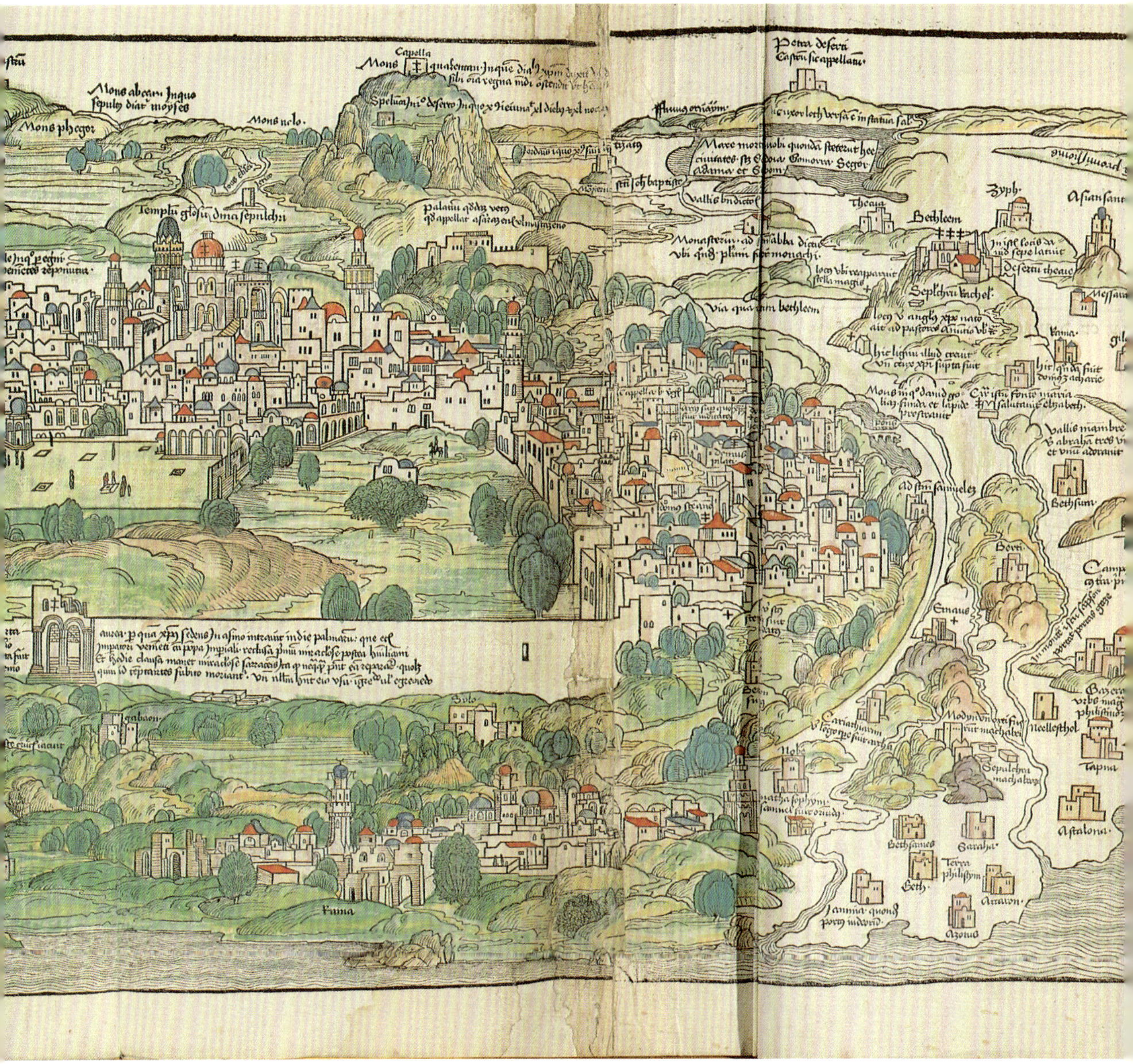

"Civitas Iherusalem" [City of Jerusalem] (detail). Bernhard von Breydenbach. *Peregrinatio in terram sanctam* [Journey to the Holy Land]. Mainz, 1486. Gift of the Burndy Library.

This work is believed to be the earliest printed travel book to contain illustrations. The artist, Erhard Reuwich, accompanied Breydenbach, and his work is based on firsthand observation.

Cultural and Social History

OVER THE YEARS SPECIAL COLLECTIONS HAS GATHERED unusual and intriguing materials in cultural and social history to support Smithsonian exhibitions and research.

Rudolph Ackermann, editor and publisher. *Repository of arts, literature, commerce, manufactures, fashions, and politics.* London, 1809–15.

Ladies' magazines published in the late 1700s were short-lived, but they reached a newly recognized audience. The Repository *was described by the historian of book illustration David Bland as a factory for color-plate illustration. Each issue featured six "embellishments," including pictures of eminent persons, furniture design, costume, and architectural views. The sample swatches of cloth in each issue are of particular interest to designers and to textile and costume historians.*

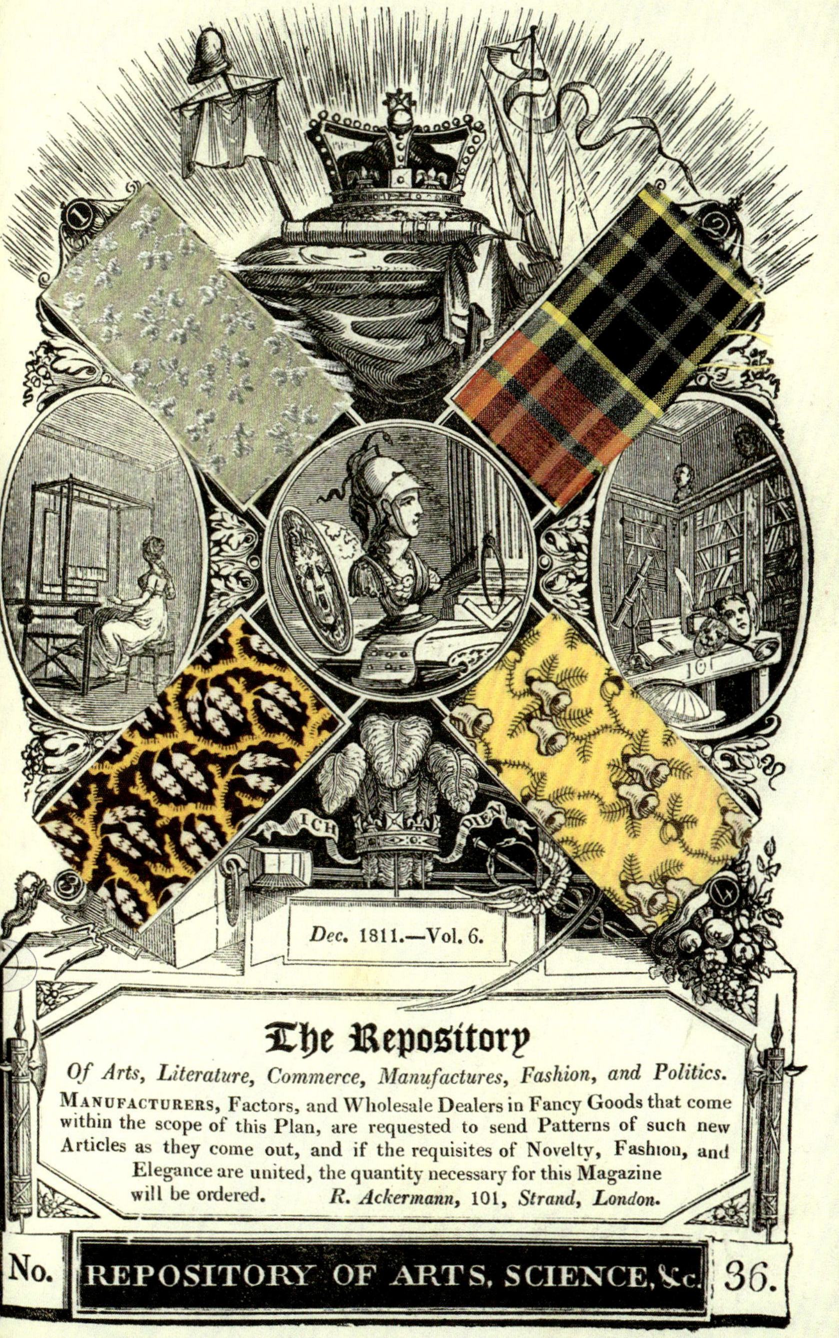

The Repository

Of Arts, Literature, Commerce, Manufactures, Fashion, and Politics.

MANUFACTURERS, Factors, and Wholesale Dealers in Fancy Goods that come within the scope of this Plan, are requested to send Patterns of such new Articles as they come out, and if the requisites of Novelty, Fashion, and Elegance are united, the quantity necessary for this Magazine will be ordered. *R. Ackermann*, 101, *Strand, London.*

No. REPOSITORY OF ARTS, SCIENCE, &c. 36.

American History and Life

In the 1950s the Libraries began to collect books of manners and etiquette and costume design, along with itinerant builders' pattern books and nineteenth-century cookbooks. Other primary source materials located in Special Collections are works pertaining to American architecture, building materials and construction, furnishings, and costume.

Health and medical topics, particularly pharmacy, are well represented. The joint American Pharmaceutical Association and Bristol-Myers Squibb donation includes medical formularies, pharmaceutical price lists, and manuscript family recipe books which provide a glimpse into daily life from the 1600s to the 1800s.

Through gifts and transfers, the Libraries has accumulated a working collection in African American history and culture, including publications of abolitionists and major African American writers. The holdings include the first known cookbook by an African American, Robert Roberts's *The House Servant's Directory* (1827), and Benjamin Banneker's *Pennsylvania, Delaware, Maryland and Virginia almanack and ephemeris for the year of our Lord 1792.* Called the "African Astronomer," Banneker was the nation's first well-known African American scientist.

Phillis Wheatley. *Poems on various subjects, religious and moral.* London and Boston, 1773.

Brought to Boston as a slave, Wheatley was educated and freed by her owners. Remembered as the first African-American poet, she died in poverty, aged thirty-one, in 1784.

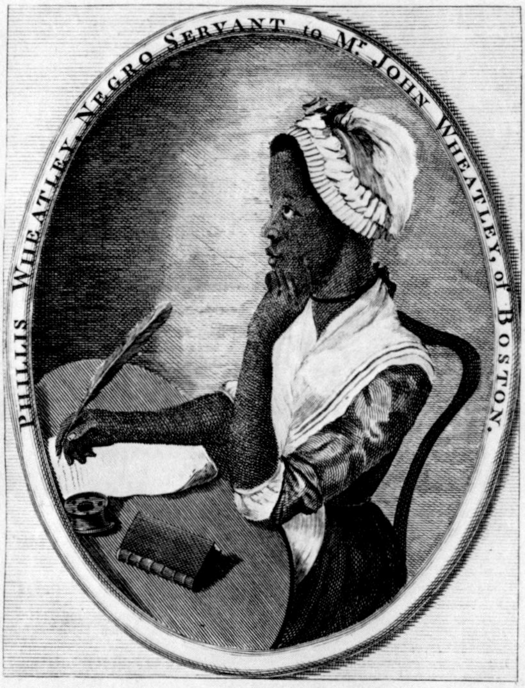

Published according to Act of Parliament, Sept.r 1, 1773 by Arch.d Bell. Bookseller No. 8 near the Saracens Head Aldgate.

POEMS ON VARIOUS SUBJECTS, RELIGIOUS AND MORAL.

BY

PHILLIS WHEATLEY,

NEGRO SERVANT to Mr. JOHN WHEATLEY, of BOSTON, in NEW ENGLAND.

LONDON:
Printed for A. BELL, Bookseller, Aldgate; and sold by Messrs. COX and BERRY, King-Street, *BOSTON.*
M DCC LXXIII.

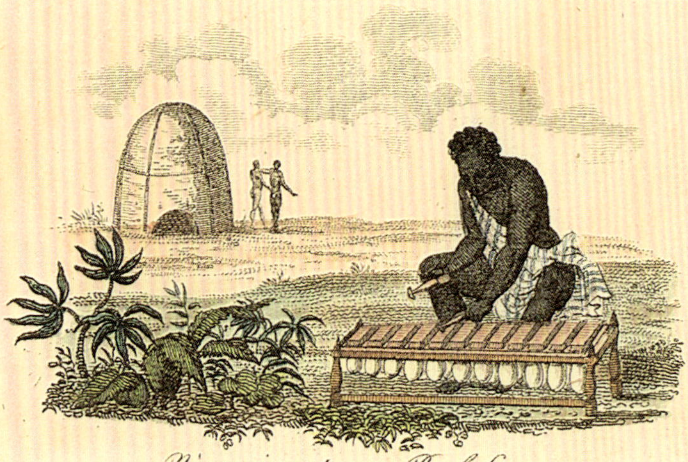

Nègre jouant au Balafo.

African Art

When the Museum of African Art became part of the Smithsonian Institution in 1979, the Libraries began to develop its library, building upon the work of Warren H. Robbins (founder and first director of the museum), for whom the library is named. Selected rare books from the seventeenth century onward provide research resources for the scholar, among them François Froger's *Relation d'un voyage fait en 1695 . . . aux côtes d'Afrique* [Account of a voyage made in 1695 . . . to the coasts of Africa] (Paris, 1698) and Thomas Edward Bowdich's *Mission from Cape Coast Castle to Ashantee* (London, 1819).

"Nègre jouant au Balafo" [Negro playing the balafo]. René Claude Geoffroy de Villeneuve. *Afrique, ou histoire, mœurs, usages et coutumes des Africains: Le Sénégal* [Africa, or the history, manners, customs of the Africans: Senegal]. Paris, 1814.

Villeneuve described customs, traditions, and religious beliefs of the Wolof, Mandingo, Serer, and Fulani peoples. He lived for twenty years in Senegal and became fluent in the Wolof language.

The Tourist.

You see him over all the world
Wherever you may go,
And when he starts upon a trip
He's always laughing so.
Sometimes he makes a little joke
And then he winks his eye,
Sometimes the toothache troubles him
And swells his cheek up high.
He puts his eye-glass in his eye
And smokes a big cigar,
And never says a word except
"I wonder where we are."
He always wears such funny clothes
Abroad in foreign lands,
And when the people speak to him
He seldom understands.

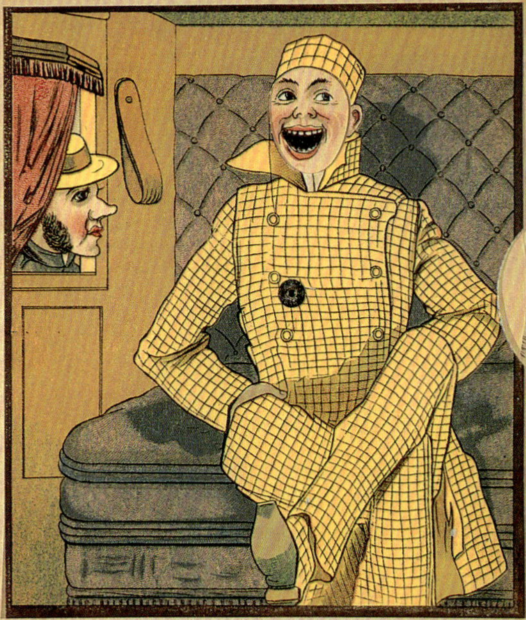

Juvenile Literature

Children's books are housed in several rare book locations in the Libraries. The Comegys family library, housed in the Dibner Library, retains a small but much-used selection of 1880s children's annuals and storybooks, including *Our Young Folks* and several stories by Juliana H. Ewing illustrated by Ralph Caldecott (for whom the Caldecott medal for children's book illustration is named). The Comegys library was assembled in the nineteenth century by a wealthy Presbyterian family of Dutch descent living in Philadelphia and is an exemplar of the literary tastes of its times.

The Cooper-Hewitt National Design Museum Branch Library's Bradley Room has two juvenile collections, one a selection of late nineteenth-century European children's books notable for their design, layout, and illustration, and the other a collection of pop-up books published from 1880 to recent years, acquired in two major gifts from Daniel J. Mason and John H. Mahey respectively. The Admiral DeWitt Clinton Ramsey Room in the National Air and Space Museum Branch Library boasts collections of boys' adventure series and Big Little Books featuring flying aces and fantasies of space travel and rockets.

"The Tourist." *Turn again, turn again!* [Germany, between 1880 and 1915?]

Transformations, that is, books with panels which slide between sheets and change the images, were favorite toy books. Many were produced in Germany.

Anthropology

ANTHROPOLOGY IS THE STUDY OF HUMANKIND FROM ITS EARLIEST traces. As a discrete subject of inquiry, its roots are found in the last two centuries of Western thought and development. However, concern with human biological evolution and cultural change can be traced back into antiquity.

An early important contributor in the search to understand human diversity is Johann Friedrich Blumenbach (1752–1840). Active in the fields of medicine, comparative anatomy, and natural history, he laid the groundwork for race classification based on anatomical measurement in his thesis *De genera humani varietate nativa* [On the natural variety of mankind]. This work is represented in Special Collections by a 1776 edition; part of the Burndy Library donation.

Other early studies of note in the development of anthropology are Charles White's 1799 *An Account of the Regular Gradation in Man and in Different Animals and Vegetables from the Former to the Latter,* a 1779 edition of Henry Home, Lord Kames's *Sketches of the History of Man,* and comparative anatomical work by Peter Camper in the nineteenth century. The Libraries' holdings also provide researchers with works on physiognomy from the Renaissance, Edward Tyson's late seventeenth-century study of the chimpanzee, the work of Johann Caspar Lavater (1741–1801), and books on phrenology.

The Smithsonian Institution played a key role in the development of American anthropology. Its ethnological and archaeological work is broadly based. The Libraries' Special Collections materials reflect the breadth of these endeavors with particular strengths in Native American studies, missionary publications, and Central and Latin America.

Wilhelm A. Graah. *Undersögelses-reise til östkysten af Grönland* [Narrative of an expedition to the east coast of Greenland]. Copenhagen, 1832.

Greenland Eskimo man kayaker dancing while women umiak rowers prepare food in European pots over Eskimo stoves in W. A. Graah's winter quarters during his 1829–30 expedition along the east coast of Greenland. Gift of Ruth Lawson Webb.

Pl. VII.

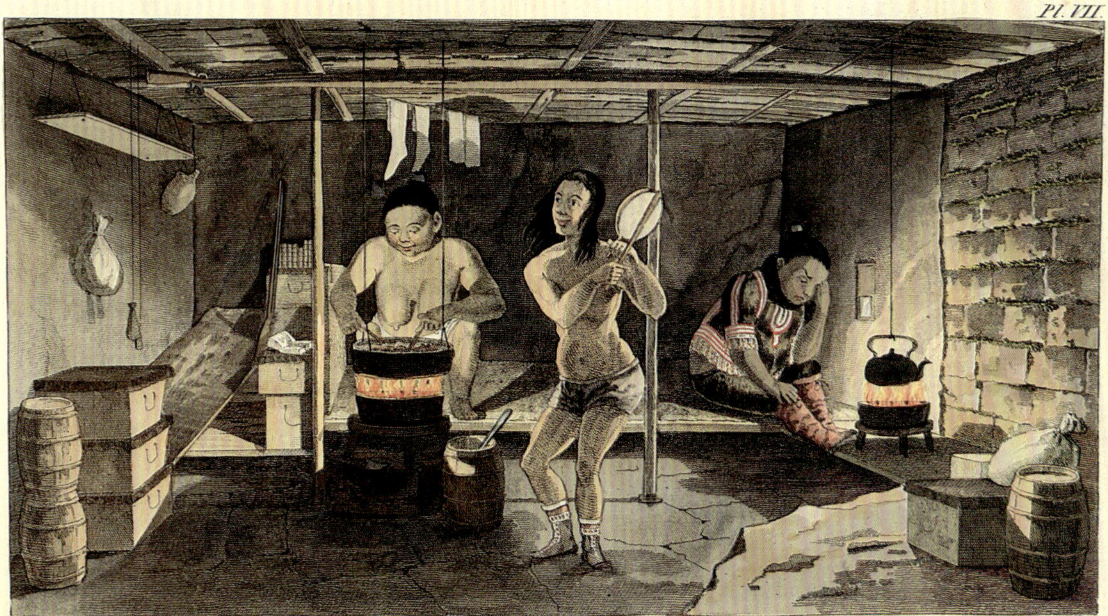

Tegnet af H.G.F. Holm efter en Skizze af Graah. Stukket af I. Holm.

Native American Studies

The Institution's long tradition of leadership in the study of Native American culture, language, and history is rooted in the work of the Bureau of American Ethnology (1879–1965) and its concern for documenting what it saw as the rapidly disappearing lifestyles of Native Americans. Materials from its library, now merged with that of the Department of Anthropology, constitute one of the most significant components of the Libraries' Special Collections. Among these works are George Catlin's colorfully illustrated accounts, in word and image, of the customs and manners of western tribal life, Thomas Lorraine McKenney and James Hall's splendid color-lithographed portraits of Native American tribal leaders who served as emissaries to Washington, and a full set of Edward S. Curtis's *The North American Indian* (Seattle, 1907–30).

"Rant Che Wai Me—Female Flying Pigeon." Thomas Lorraine McKenney and James Hall. *History of the Indian tribes of North America, with biographical sketches and anecdotes of the principal chiefs.* Philadelphia, 1836–44.

Thomas McKenney established his Archives of the American Indian in Washington in 1818, acquiring many of Thomas Bird King's portraits of visiting Native American delegations to the government. Rant Che Wai Me was the wife of Pahoochee, chief of an Ioway tribe. She accompanied the Ioway delegation to Washington, where this portrait was probably made.

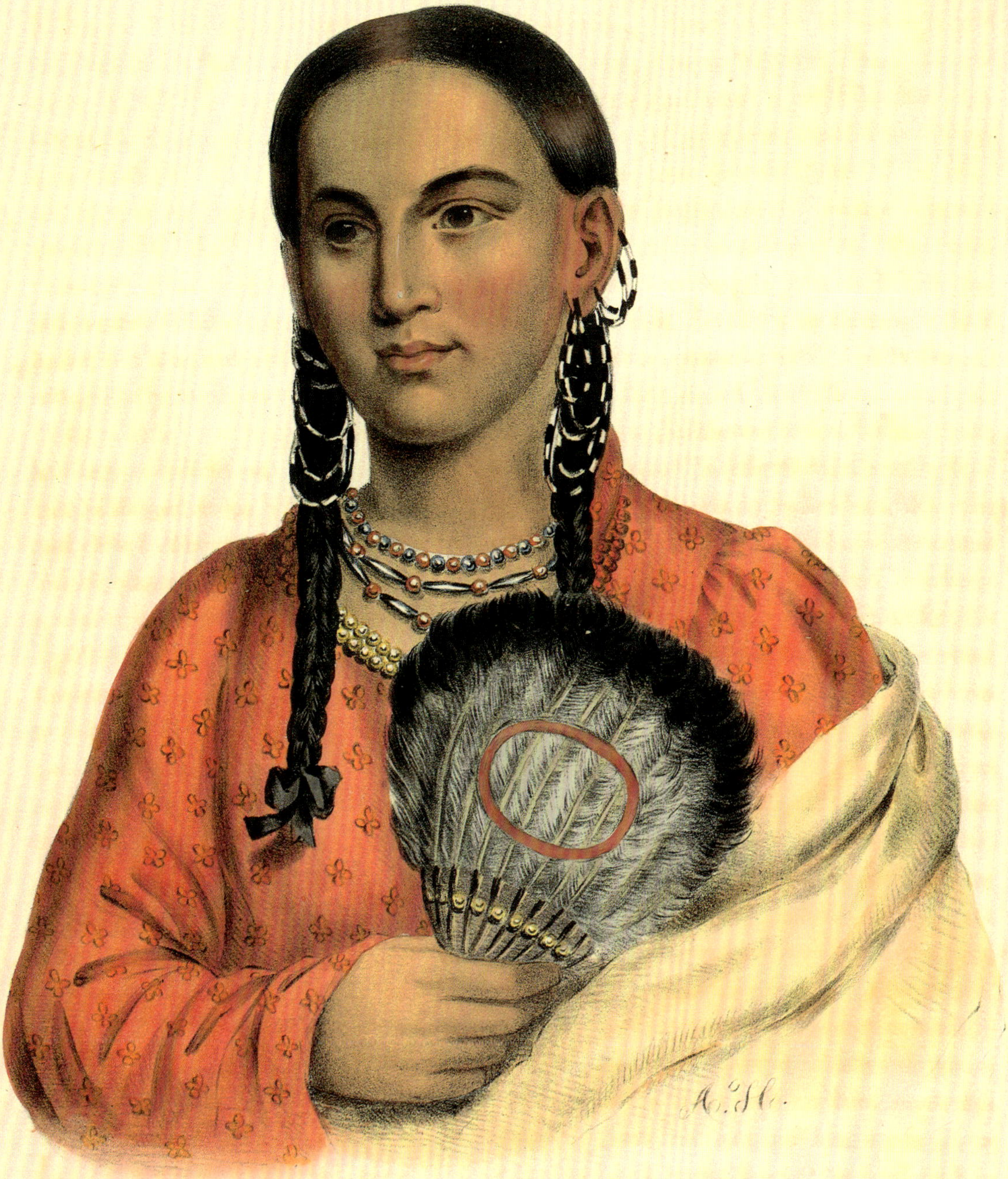

RANT CHE WAI ME

FEMALE FLYING PIGEON.

PUBLISHED BY F. W. GREENOUGH, PHILAD^A.

Drawn Printed & Coloured at I.T. Bowen's Lithographic Establishment No. 94 Walnut St.

THE CHEROKEE MESSENGER.

ᏣᎳᎩ ᎠᏥᏅᏏᏛ.

VOL. I. AUGUST, 1844. NO. 1.

ᏑᏕᏘᏴᏛ ᏧᎦᎴᏴᏔᏅᎯ I. ᎦᎶᏂ, 1844. ᎠᏎᎯᎲᎢ 1.

Translation of Genesis into the Cherokee Language.

ᏗᏁᏢᏔᏅᎯ ᎪᏪᎵ ᏗᏓᎴᏂᏍᎬ ᎼᏏ ᎤᏬᏪᎳᏅᎯ.

ᎥᏝ ᏔᎵᏁ ᏗᎦᎴᏴᏙᏗ ᎠᏂ ᏲᏥᏰᏄᎾ ᏦᎢ ᎢᎬᏱᏱ ᎾᏯᏙᏄ ᏗᏓᎴᏂᏍᎬ ᎼᏏ ᎤᏬᏪᎳᏅᎯ, ᎦᏳᎳᏰᏃ ᎢᏄᎯᏳ ᏗᎬᏁᏢᏔᏅᎯ ᎠᎴ ᏗᎬᏰᎵᎯᏍᏔᏅᎯ ᏂᎬᎾᏛ ᎠᏂ ᏣᎳᎩᏱ.

ᎠᏯᏙᏄᎢ IV.

1 ᎠᏓᏫᏃ ᎤᏕᏙᎥᏎ ᎢᏫ ᎤᏓᎵᎢ; ᎠᎴ ᎤᏁᎵᏤᎢ, ᎠᎴ ᎤᎾᏄᎪᏫᏎ ᎨᏂ, ᎠᎴ ᎯᎠ ᏄᏪᏎᎢ, ᏱᎰᏩᏍᎩᏂ ᎠᎩᏩᏛ ᎠᏍᎦᏯ.

2 ᏔᎵᏁᏃ ᎤᎾᏄᎪᏫᏎ ᎤᏅᏟ ᎡᏈᎵ, ᎡᏈᎵᏃ ᎠᏫ ᏗᎦᏘᏯ ᎨᏎᎢ, ᎨᏂᏍᎩᏂ ᏠᎨᏏ ᏧᏄᏫᏍᏓᏁᎯ ᎨᏎᎢ.

3 ᎢᏄᎯᏳᏃ ᎢᏴᏛ ᎯᎠ ᏄᎵᏍᏔᏁᎢ, ᎨᏂ ᎤᏲᎮᎴ ᏱᎰᏩ ᎠᎵᏍᎪᎸᏔᏅᎯ ᎦᏙᎯ ᎤᏛᏒᎯ.

4 ᎡᏈᎵᏃ ᎾᏍᏉ ᎤᏲᎴ ᎤᏤᎵ ᎢᎬᏱᏱ ᏗᎨᎦᏅᏅᎯ ᎠᏫ ᎠᎴ ᎤᎵᏦᎯᏛ. ᏱᎰᏩᏃ ᏚᏓᏂᎸᏤ ᎡᏈᎵ ᎠᎴ ᎤᎵᏍᎪᎸᏔᏅᎯ.

5 ᎨᏂᏍᎩᏂ ᎠᎴ ᎤᎵᏍᎪᎸᏔᏅᎯ ᎥᏝ ᏱᏚᏓᏂᎸᏤᎢ. ᎨᏂᏃ ᎤᏣᏘ ᎤᏔᎳᏬᏎᎢ, ᎠᎴ ᏣᎦᎦᏃᏗᏱ ᎡᏔᏗ ᏄᎵᏍᏔᏁᎢ.

6 ᏱᎰᏩᏃ ᎯᎠ ᏄᏪᏎᎴ ᎨᏂ, ᎦᏙᏃ ᎢᏣᎾᏄᎭᏉ? ᎠᎴ ᎦᏙᏃ ᏤᏣᏍᏃᏗᏱ ᎡᏔᏗᏉ ᏂᎤᏍᏗ?

7 ᎢᏳᏰᏃ ᎣᏏ ᏱᏂᏣᏛᏁᎸ, ᏝᏥᏃ ᏱᏙᎦᏰᏣᏓᏂᎸᎩ? ᎣᏒᏃ ᏂᏣᏛᏁᎸᎾ ᏱᎩ, ᎠᏍᎦᎾᏰᏃ ᎦᎶᎯᏍᏗᏱᏉ ᎢᎦᏅᎦ. ᎠᎴᏃ ᏂᎯ ᎮᎲ ᏚᏁᏣᏕᏍᏗ, ᎯᏯᏓᏅᏖᎮᎵᏕᎯᏉᏃ ᎨᏎᏍᏗ.

8 ¶ ᎨᏂᏃ ᎤᎵᏃᎮᏔᏁ ᎤᏅᏟ ᎡᏈᎵ: ᎠᎴ ᎯᎠ ᏄᎵᏍᏔᏁᎢ, ᏠᎨᏏ ᎠᏁᏙᎲᎢ, ᎨᏂ ᏚᎦᏘᏄᏎ ᎤᏅᏟ ᎡᏈᎵ, ᎠᎴ ᎤᎴᎢ.

9 ᏱᎰᏩᏃ ᎯᎠ ᏄᏪᏎᎴ ᎨᏂ, ᎭᏢ, ᎡᏣᏅᏟ ᎡᏈᎵ? ᎯᎠᏃ ᏄᏪᏎᎢ, Ꮭ ᏱᏥᎦᏔᎭ: ᏥᎪᎨ ᎠᏴ ᎥᎩᏅᏟ ᏥᎦᏘᏯ?

10 ᎯᎠᏃ ᏄᏪᏎᎢ, ᎦᏙ ᏣᏛᏁᎸ? ᎦᏙᎯ ᎢᏴᏛ ᏗᎩᏁᏤ ᎡᏣᏅᏟ ᎤᎩᎬ.

11 ᎠᎴ ᎿᏉ ᎡᎶᎯ ᎡᏣᏍᎦᏨᎯ ᎨᏎᏍᏗ, ᎾᏍᎩ ᏧᏔᏩᏅ ᎡᏣᏅᏟ ᎤᎩᎬ ᏗᏦᏰᏂ ᏗᏨᏔᏅᎯ ᏥᏣᏗᏔᏏ;

12 ᎢᏳᏃ ᎦᏙᎯ ᏕᎯᏣᎩᏍᎨᏍᏗ, ᎪᎯ ᎢᏳᏓᎴᏅᏛ ᎥᏝ ᎣᏍᏛ ᏱᏣᏛᎯᏎᎮᏍᏗ; ᎠᎴ ᏣᎵᏯᏛᏉ ᎠᎴ ᎾᎭᎴᏁᎯᏉ ᎨᏎᏍᏗ ᎡᎶᎯ.

13 ᎨᏂᏃ ᎯᎠ ᏄᏪᏎᎴ ᏱᎰᏩ, (ᎡᏉᎯᏳᏉ ᏥᎩᎵᏲᎬᎢ,) ᎥᏝ ᏰᎵ ᏱᏂᏥᏍᏓᏴ, ᎾᏍᎩ ᎢᎦᎢ ᎠᎩᎩᎵᏲᎢᏍᏗᏱ.

14 ᎬᏂᏳᏉᏰᏃ, ᎪᎯ ᎢᎦ ᏍᎩᎨᎯᏓ ᎡᎶᎯ; ᎠᎴ ᏂᎯ ᏗᏣᏫᏖᏂᏓᏍᏗᏱ ᎠᏆᏗᏍᎦᎴᏍᏗ; ᎠᎴ ᎠᏆᎵᏗᏛ ᎠᎴ ᎾᎦᎴᏁᎯ ᎨᏎᏍᏗ ᎡᎶᎯ; ᎠᎴ ᎯᎠ ᏅᏓᎦᎵᏍᏔᏂ ᎾᏂᎥᏉ ᎬᎩᏩᏛᏍᎨᏍᏗ ᎬᎩᎯᎮᏍᏗ.

15 ᏱᎰᏩᏃ ᎯᎠ ᏄᏪᏎᎴᎢ, ᎢᏳᏃ ᎩᎶ ᎢᎠᎯᎮᏍᏗ ᎨᏂ, ᎦᎵᏉᎩ ᎢᏳᏩᎫᏗ ᎠᏕᏝᏤᏗ ᎨᏎᏍᏗ. ᎠᎴ ᏱᎰᏩ ᎤᏬᏪᎳᏁ ᎨᏂ, ᎾᏍᎩᏰᏃ ᎩᎶ ᏱᎬᏩᏩᏛᎲ ᎦᎬᏩᎯᏍᏗᏉ ᏂᎨᏒᎾ ᎢᏳᎵᏍᏙᏗᏱ.

16 ᎨᏂᏃ ᎿᏉ ᎤᏓᏅᏒᎴ ᏱᎰᏩ, ᎠᎴ ᏃᏗᏱ ᏧᏁᏔᏕᎢ, ᎢᏕᏂ ᎨᏒ ᏗᎧᎸᎬ ᎢᏗᏢ ᏭᏚᏳᎪᏛᎢ.

Missionary Publications

The Libraries owns one of the country's most comprehensive collections of publications by missionaries for Native Americans. Printed in small quantities, they have become very rare. In an effort to provide Indians with religious information, the missionaries transcribed Native American languages into written form, often using the Bible, catechisms, and spellers as texts. Examples are the Ioway and Sac Mission Press's *An Ioway grammar, illustrating the principles of the language used by the Ioway, Otoe, and Missouri Indians* (1848) and the Book of Common Prayer in Mohawk (1842), Chippewa (1853), Dakota (1865), and several other languages. These have become invaluable linguistic and historical sources. Many were brought to the Smithsonian by James Constance Pilling, the great bibliographer of Native American languages.

The Cherokee Messenger. [Cherokee, Iowa, 1844–46.] Shown: first page of issue no. 1, August 1844.

Published by the Baptist Mission Press, the Messenger *began an ambitious program to provide a translation of the Bible in Cherokee. News of missionary activities in Indian territories and reservations filled the issues. This issue belonged to Otis Mason, first curator of Ethnology at the Bureau of American Ethnology.*

Central and Latin America

Edward King, Viscount Kingsborough's stately *Antiquities of Mexico* (London, 1831–48) was one of the first published facsimiles of Central American codices (nine volumes). The publisher was Robert Havell, who also published J. J. Audubon's double elephant folio edition of *The Birds of America.*

In the late 1880s Joseph Florimond, the Duc de Loubat, and other archaeological enthusiasts funded the production of facsimiles of the few surviving original Mesoamerican manuscripts, which were by then scattered among a number of European repositories. These scarce fragments—which Florimond and others reproduced using the new techniques of color lithography and photography—constitute a principal resource for study of Precolumbian cultures of the Americas. Florimond donated many of his facsimiles to the Institution as they were published; these early limited editions are now scarce and often fragile.

Vatican Library. Mss. Cod. vat. 3773. Il manoscritto messicano vaticano 3773 [The Vatican Mexican manuscript 3773]. Rome, 1896.

This prehispanic codex, probably from the Mixteca, covers calendrical, astronomical, and mythological subjects. It begins with a tonalpohualli, *a religious calendar of 260 days; other sections depict complex rituals and detailed representations of numerous central Mexican deities.*

(46)

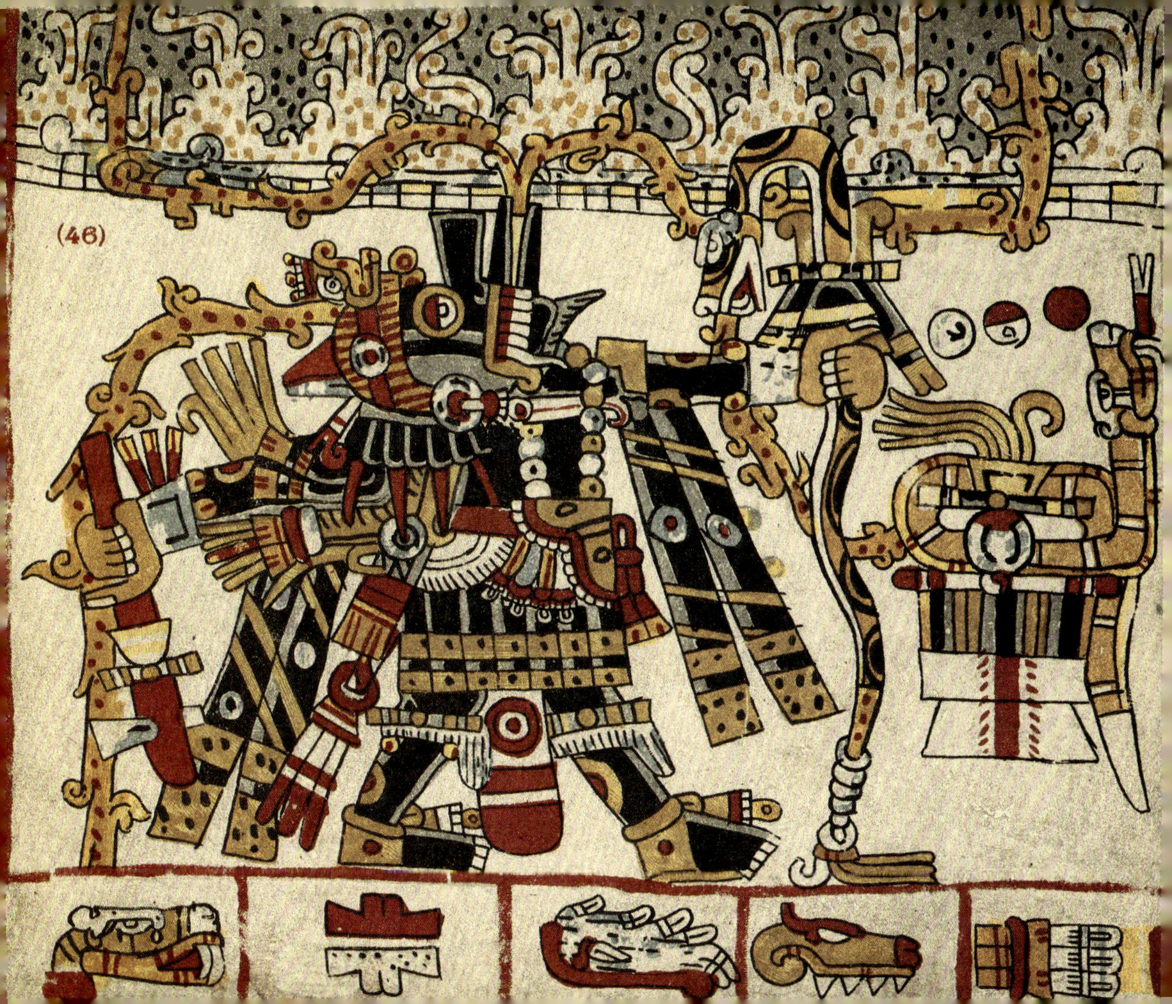

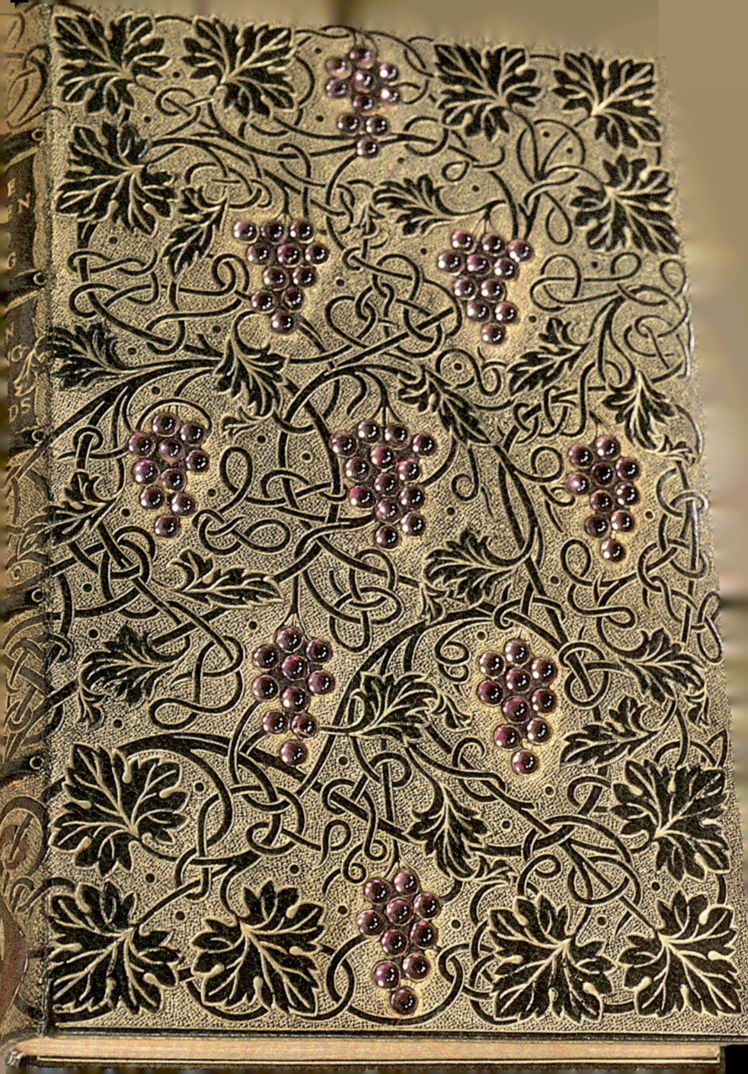

Decorative Arts

WHEN THE COOPER-HEWITT NATIONAL DESIGN MUSEUM opened to the public as part of the Smithsonian in 1976, it brought to the Institution a library with major resources in the history of American design and its European origins. This branch library supports course-related work of graduate students from the Parsons School of Design. A steady stream of gifts and bequests, including collections from Dorothy Nickerson on the history of color, Phelps Warren on glass, and Richard Barrett on jewelry, have enriched the collections.

John Addington Symonds. *Wine, women and song; mediaeval Latin students' songs now first translated into English verse.* London, 1884. Gift of Mrs. Katherine Epler.

This work contains selected translations from the Carmina burana *[The songs of Beuren], a thirteenth-century collection of secular Latin songs discovered in the Monastery of Benedicktbeuren in Bavaria in 1803. The Libraries' copy of this edition was handsomely bound by Sangorski and Sutcliffe. The covers and doublures of green morocco are lavishly stippled and tooled in gold. Clustered amethysts on the front cover represent bunches of grapes.*

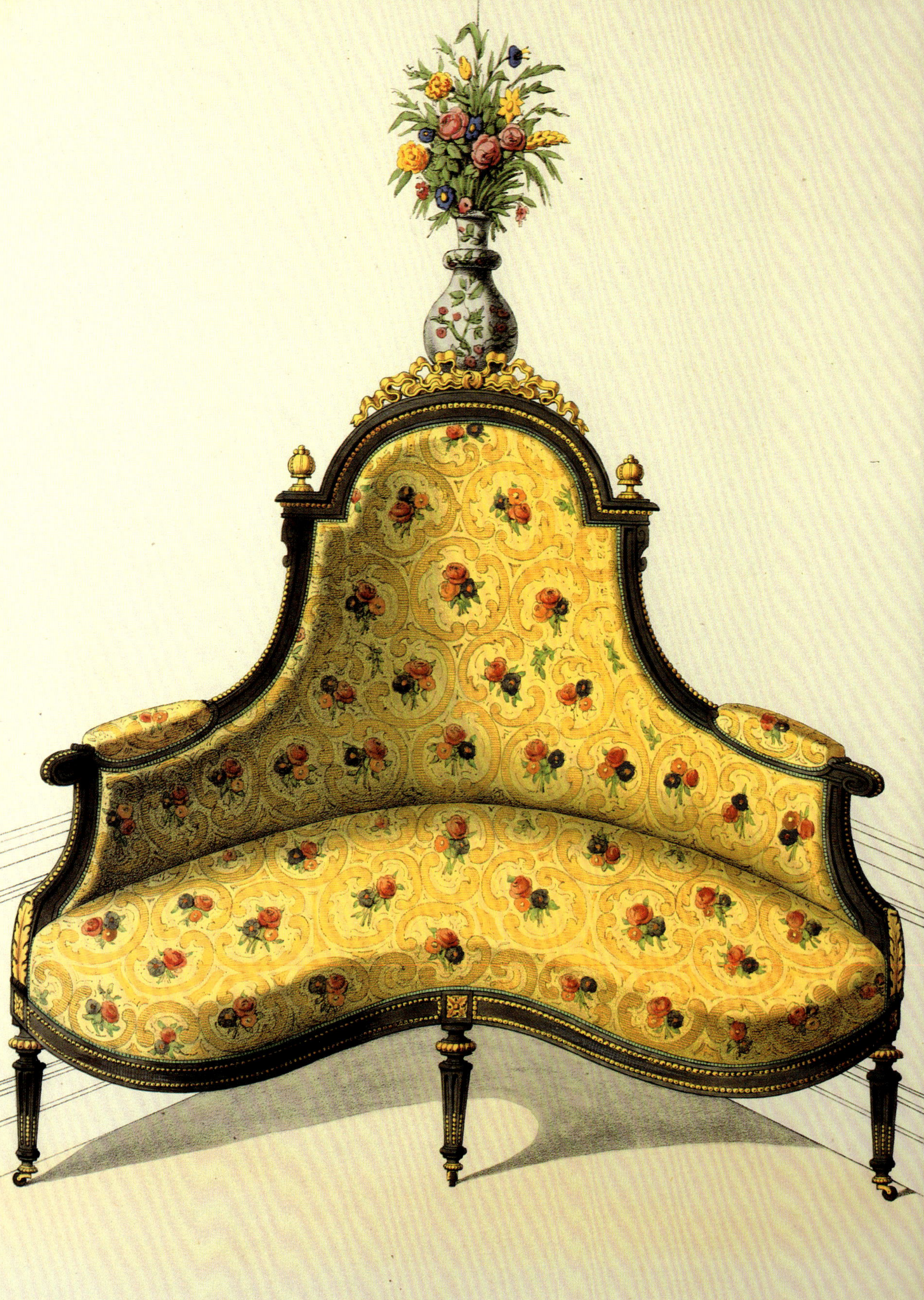

Causeuse d'Encoignure

Bois noir et Cuivres dorés.

Interior Design

Robert Adams's *Works in architecture* (London, 1773–82) and Thomas Hope's *Household furniture and interior design* (London, 1807) enable researchers to follow the development and transfer of decoration and fashion in both the New and Old World. Rare periodicals such as the *Journal des dames et des modes* [Journal of women and fashion] (1912–14) and *Le garde meuble* [The furniture repository] (1839–1900) provide rare pictorial resources. Donald Deskey and other major designers have donated their papers to support investigations of the development of interior design as a profession in the twentieth century. The Cooper-Hewitt National Design Museum Branch Library also has valuable materials for the study of textiles, clothing, furniture, and household wares.

"Corner love seat [ca. 1890]." *Le garde meuble* [The furniture repository]. Paris (1839–1935).

The publisher of this periodical, Guimard, promoted French styles, concentrating especially on furniture for living and dining rooms. His catalogs were a great influence on American interior design. The title refers to the office established by Louis XIV for royal furnishings. Purchase of Le garde meuble, *volumes 1–3 (1839–1900), was made possible by funds from a Smithsonian Women's Committee grant, funds from the Cooper-Hewitt National Design Museum, and from the Smithsonian Institution Libraries.*

Landscape Design

Research materials for landscape design are housed in four branch library locations, the Horticulture Branch Library, Botany Branch Library, Cooper-Hewitt National Design Museum Branch Library, and the Dibner Library. These resources include classical studies like Humphry Repton's *Observations on the theory and practice of landscape gardening* (London, 1803) and his *Design for the pavilion of Brighton* (London, 1808). The publications of Andrew Jackson Downing, an architect, horticulturist, and landscape designer who had a significant impact on gardening and residential architecture of the 1840s and 1850s, are also well represented.

Humphry Repton. *The landscape gardening and landscape architecture of the late Humphrey [sic] Repton. . . . A new edition . . . by J. C. Loudon.* London, 1840.

This hand-colored illustration shows the effect of designing a landscape at Wentworth to achieve the impression of a river.

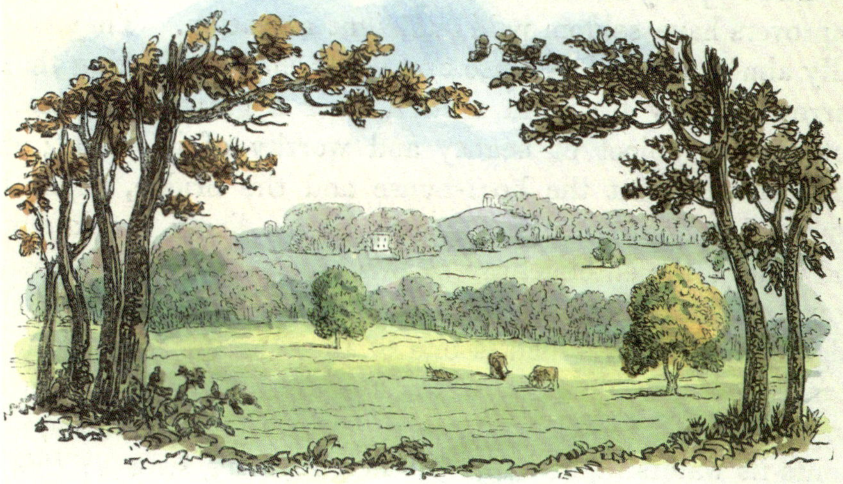

[Fig. 54. View in the park at Wentworth, before certain trees were removed, which exclude a view of the water from the approach.]

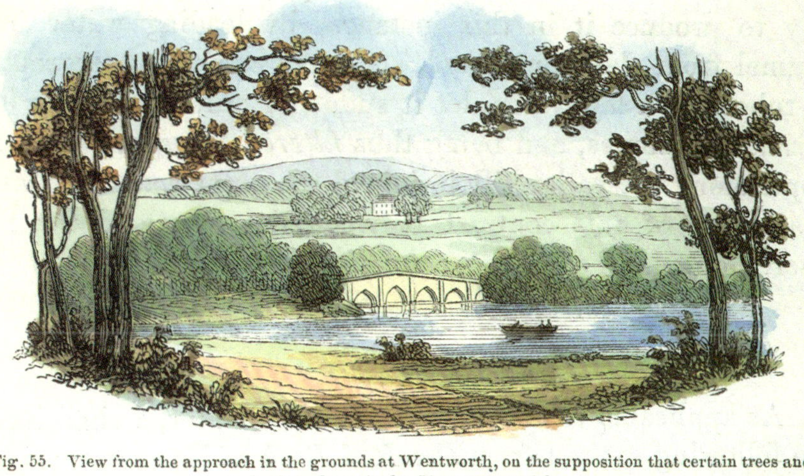

[Fig. 55. View from the approach in the grounds at Wentworth, on the supposition that certain trees and bushes, shewn in fig. 54, are removed.]

COLOPHON

This book was composed in Monotype Bulmer, based on types cut by William Martin for the Shakspeare Printing Office of William Bulmer. Dedicated to the ideals of fine typography, Martin and Bulmer collaborated on the nine-volume "Boydell Shakspeare" (1792–1802), as well as Poems of Goldsmith and Parnell *(1795) and* The Chase *by William Somerville (1796).*

Martin's font combines beauty with functionality and anticipates the Modern style of Bodoni while retaining qualities from the Transitional style of Baskerville. This digital version of Bulmer, first released in 1994, was redrawn in the Monotype Type Drawing Office by Ron Carpenter following a study of Bulmer's printed works and extensive research into hot metal versions of the 1930s.

Rare Books and Special Collections in the Smithsonian Institution Libraries *was designed by Robert L. Wiser of Meadows & Wiser in Washington, D.C., and printed by The Stinehour Press in Lunenburg, Vermont, on 100-pound Potlatch Vintage Velvet.*

"*Anthremus varius* Fabr." Georg Wolfgang Franz Panzer. *Faunæ insectorum germanicæ initia* [The elements of the German insect fauna]. Nuremberg, 1796–1813.

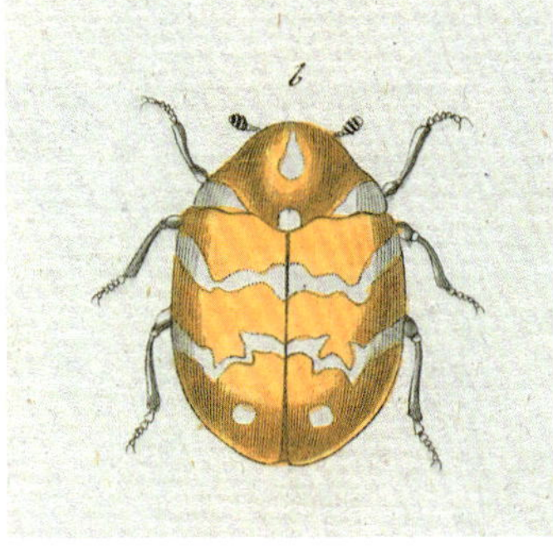